*American Princess*

# *American Princess*

## THE LOVE STORY OF

## Meghan Markle and Prince Harry

### LESLIE CARROLL

*wm*

WILLIAM MORROW
*An Imprint of HarperCollinsPublishers*

HarperCollins books may be purchased for educational, business, or sales promotional use. For information, please email the Special Markets Department at SPsales@harpercollins.com.

FIRST EDITION

Designed by Diahann Sturge

Library of Congress Cataloging-in-Publication Data has been applied for.

ISBN 978-0-06-285945-7

18 19 20 21 22    DIX/LSC    10 9 8 7 6 5 4 3 2 1

*For Scott—my husband*—my *prince*

*With fame comes opportunity, but it also includes responsibility—to advocate and share, to focus less on glass slippers and more on pushing through glass ceilings. And, if I'm lucky enough, to inspire.*

—MEGHAN MARKLE

*The world is changing as everybody knows, and we've changed with it. I think everybody can see that.*

—PRINCE HARRY OF WALES

# Contents

## Foreword

### This Scept'red Aisle

Once upon a time—right up to the dawn of the twentieth century, in fact—royal marriages were arranged relationships, peace treaties that secured borders and cemented political alliances. Those who wanted to marry for love were considered to have abrogated their duties.

And yet the most modern love story in the history of the thousand-year-old British monarchy began in a similar way to many royal matches of centuries past: as a setup.

On the cloudy afternoon of November 27, 2017, Prince Harry of Wales, then fifth in line to the throne, descended a series of flagstone steps into Kensington Palace's Sunken Garden with his beautiful raven-haired fiancée. They were there for the obligatory photo session that followed Clarence House's official announcement of their engagement a few hours earlier. The gray waters of the reflecting pool mirrored their images variously holding hands, arms entwined, heads inclined toward each other, a pair of terrestrial swans in a mating dance, able to read and anticipate each other's body language. The couple's radiant smiles more than made up for the absence of the sun. With no coat over his royal blue suit, Harry must not have felt the autumnal nip in the air. Wearing a belted white trench coat, his intended bride, Meghan Markle, was already breaking royal protocol by not wearing pantyhose.

That fashion statement alone was enough of a clue that Meghan was already doing things differently; and their frequent and public displays of affection are another hint that she and Harry already are and will be like no other couple the monarchy has ever seen.

Their fateful blind date had taken place less than seventeen months earlier; and in the intervening time they had been as inseparable as they could manage for two people who lived on different continents and whose individual professional commitments kept them occupied nearly every day. Meghan was no nubile foreign princess waiting to be told which dynastic marriage awaited her, or a teenage English rose with little experience of the world.

Meghan Markle *is* a foreigner. But even a generation ago, her marriage to Harry would have been unimaginable.

Cut to a soggy polo match at Smith's Lawn during one rainy day at Windsor in 1970. As the story goes, a five-foot-eight-inch blonde bearing a remarkable resemblance to the Prince of Wales's childhood nanny sauntered up to him through the mud; and with supreme confidence, complimented his pony. "That's a fine animal, sir! I thought you played wonderfully well." Having won Prince Charles's attention, on their second encounter she blatantly propositioned him. "My great-grandmother and your great-great-grandfather were lovers: how about it?"

Camilla Shand's father was a courtier with the somewhat priapic title "Silver Stick." The ancestress she'd alluded to was Alice Keppel, known as "La Favorita," mistress for more than a dozen years to Edward VII—who'd had to be bodily removed from the dying king's bedside by command of the queen, who wanted her rival out of sight.

Queen Elizabeth's oldest son fell head over heels for Camilla, and the pair dated before Charles entered the Royal Navy. But he never proposed, and Camilla was unwilling to wait for him. In 1973, she wed Andrew Parker Bowles, a captain of the household cavalry eight years her senior. But at the time she and Charles began dating, even if the Prince of Wales had evinced no fear of commitment, Buckingham Palace would have been unwilling to accept Camilla as a suitable bride. Despite the fact that her father was a courtier and she'd attended good schools, the Shands were not considered aristocratic enough for Camilla to be future-queen-of-England material. Moreover, Camilla was not a virgin.

Queen Elizabeth's own mother, Elizabeth Bowes-Lyon, was not royal. But *her* father was an earl and she was as pure as the driven snow when she married the then–Duke of York in 1923. When she was still the heir apparent, in 1947 Queen Elizabeth had wed a foreign royal, her fourth cousin Prince Philip of Greece and Denmark; but theirs was a love match. Moreover, in the wake of World War I, when most European monarchies had been relegated to the history books, it was no longer necessary to cement foreign alliances for political gain.

Yet to the Windsors, even in 1981, it was still important for the bride of the Prince of Wales, the heir to the throne, to pass the purity test.

Enter Lady Diana Spencer, the youngest daughter of the 8th Earl Spencer. Her pedigree was older, far posher—and more English—than Charles's. In 1603, King James I had created the 1st Baron Spencer, and the title was upgraded to an earldom by George III in 1765. The Palace determined that "Shy Di," a blushing, virginal kindergarten teacher, would make the perfect match for the Prince of Wales. The reader knows the rest of the story, of course.

Prince William, Charles and Diana's elder son, met the girl of his dreams, Catherine Middleton, during their freshman year at the University of St. Andrews in Scotland. Catherine, a willowy brunette with incomparable poise, charm, and athleticism, came from an upper-middle-class home: her father had been a British Airways flight dispatcher; and her mother, Carole, was a stewardess. Later, the online party planning business that Carole launched as an in-home start-up skyrocketed into a multimillion-dollar industry.

After cohabitating for the better part of a decade-long courtship, William and Catherine finally married on April 29, 2011. It was the first time in three hundred and fifty years that an heir to the British throne had wed a female commoner without a patrician pedigree.

So much for the hard-boiled rules handed down to Charles four decades earlier that he must marry a virgin from an aristocratic family.

Now Charles and Diana's younger son, Prince Harry, for years the most eligible bachelor in the world, the lovable, mischievous "bad boy" of the Windsors, is about to smash every taboo regarding royal marriages—and more.

Rebel, rakehell, rule breaker. Soldier, prince, private man: there's a little bit of his royal forebears in Harry, including those with a fondness for divorcées and actresses. But there is so much more that is unique and different about his choice of Meghan Markle to be his wife than there is in common with his ancestors' liaisons.

After several years of devoting his life to military service as well as to numerous philanthropic causes that are dear to his heart, Harry is ready to settle down, most likely to continue his charitable efforts, with a beautiful and spirited soulmate by his side.

She attended a Catholic school, although she was not raised a Catholic.

She is most certainly a commoner. A professional actress, in fact. For centuries, actresses, viewed as no better than tavern wenches, weren't even considered acceptable as royal *mistresses*.

She's divorced.

She's also biracial.

And furthermore, Meghan Markle is not even British.

A British prince chose to marry a biracial divorced American actress.

The last time a British royal insisted on wedding an American divorcée, it nearly provoked a constitutional crisis.

In 1934, when the future Edward VIII was still Prince of Wales, he fell wildly in love with the homely, brittle Wallis Warfield Simpson, a Baltimore belle who was on her second marriage. Their extramarital affair remained just as passionate when Edward became king in January 1936; but in that era the British press did not report about the royal family's personal lives. Therefore, Edward's subjects never knew that Wallis was still married during the first few years of her affair with Edward; and that the king very likely—and illegally—colluded in getting Wallis her divorce from Ernest Simpson.

The public also had no idea that the government had been secretly compiling information on both Wallis and Edward, and was keenly aware of their Nazi and pro-Fascist sympathies. MI6, Britain's equivalent of the CIA, knew that the feckless sovereign left the contents of his red dispatch boxes lying about; and they suspected that he might have shared some of the highly sensitive information both with Wallis and with their aristocratic cadre of pro-Reich cronies. Water stains on the papers indicated that some documents had even been used as cocktail coasters!

With Hitler on the rise across the Channel, a Nazi puppet on Britain's throne would have been a disaster for democracy.

As a way of removing an existential threat to the nation, Prime Minister Stanley Baldwin reminded His Majesty that ever since the reign of Henry VIII, the English sovereign is also the Defender of the Faith and Supreme Governor of the Church of England—a church that in the 1930s refused to recognize divorce. As king, Edward could never wed Wallis, because in the eyes of the Anglican Church she was still considered married to her second husband, Ernest Aldrich Simpson. If His Majesty nonetheless wished to marry Wallis, then he could no longer remain on the throne. If Edward stubbornly chose to remain king *and* marry his paramour in spite of his government's wishes, they would resign en masse, resulting in a constitutional crisis.

Faced with the most difficult decision of his life, the man who was bred in the bone to choose *duty above all else* chose love instead. On December 11, 1936, at 1:52 Greenwich Mean Time, Edward VIII made history when he became the first British monarch to voluntarily relinquish the crown.

Known as the Abdication Crisis, Edward VIII's abandonment of the throne for Wallis Simpson—in shorthand, an American divorcée—sent a shock wave through the Windsor dynasty that reverberated for decades. As a result, the current monarch, Elizabeth II, found herself in direct succession to the throne. In the wake of Edward VIII's complete dereliction, her father, the shy, stammering, chain-smoking Duke of York, became king, taking the name George VI.

In 1937, Edward, then titled Duke of Windsor, married the twice-divorced Wallis in France. But to the rest of the family, his new duchess would always be "that woman," the root cause of every bit of angst visited upon the reluctant George VI for the entirety of his reign.

And now, an *American divorcée*—a phrase that in itself sent shudders through the Windsor dynasty for nearly three quarters of a century—is about to marry Queen Elizabeth's grandson.

This book celebrates the once unthinkable, once impermissible royal love story of Prince Henry of Wales and Meghan Markle.

A love story that will change the face of the British monarchy forever.

To understand why and how Harry and Meghan's relationship—and royal marriage—makes history, defying centuries of arcane rules and traditions, it's important to see how far the British monarchy has come since another redheaded Harry—Henry VIII—first, irrevocably, changed its face.

## Prince Harry of Wales

Born September 15, 1984

-and-

## Meghan Markle

Born August 4, 1981

# Childe Harry

Oh, God, it's a boy. And he's even got red hair."

According to that boy's mother, Diana, Princess of Wales, those were his father Prince Charles's first words, spoken in hurtful alarm on seeing his newborn baby in Diana's arms.

Because she knew "Charles always wanted a girl," Diana admitted to her biographer, Andrew Morton, that for the sake of marital harmony she had never told her husband about the results of her pregnancy scan, and carried the secret of Harry's gender until the day he was born. On the misty late summer morning of September 15, 1984, one week shy of her projected due date, Diana awoke in her bed at Windsor Castle, but she realized she had better hightail it to London.

It was time. She and Charles departed Windsor at six-thirty A.M., arriving an hour later at the Lindo Wing of St. Mary's Hospital, Paddington, where Diana had given birth to her first child, Prince William, on June 21, 1982.

For her first six hours of labor she read a book while Charles, fetchingly dressed in a hospital gown, fed her ice chips. It was a cozy domestic scene.

Prince Henry Charles Albert David arrived at four-twenty P.M., delivered by George Parker, the same obstetrician who had brought William into the world. It should have been one of the happiest hours of the Waleses' lives.

After all, the day little blond *William* was born, when a reporter asked Charles if the infant resembled him, the prince had joked self-effacingly, "No, he's lucky enough not to."

But with son number two, his father's first reaction was cruel.

Meanwhile, downstairs in Praed Street, a crowd of three hundred well-wishers, comprised of civilians and members of the press, had waited for hours outside the Lindo Wing's redbrick facade for news of the royal birth. They were so collectively excited by the announcement that the Princess of Wales had given the family a second son that a distracted motorist smashed his vehicle into an ambulance.

Two forty-two-gun salutes ripped the air, fired simultaneously from the Tower of London and Hyde Park. A town crier clad in scarlet with a plumed hat strolled in front of the hospital bearing a scroll; he then proclaimed the official announcement of the prince's birth like a performer from a cheesy Renaissance faire. *How quaint and traditional!* thought some television viewers. As it turned out, the town crier had been hired by a Japanese TV company to add a bit of color to the event.

As an aside, a different faux town crier, Tony Appleton, whose scarlet doublet bears a violet badge that reads *Royalist Town Crier*, announced Meghan and Harry's engagement on November 27, 2017, and has voluntarily shown up at the births of the Cambridge heirs and other Windsor milestones.

A town crier was a charming touch, but the fourth grandchild to Elizabeth II was not born into a charmed household.

Diana, who had insisted on wearing sexy maternity clothes in order to please her husband, said of his gut reaction to little Harry, "Something inside me closed off."

And rather than embracing this little "miracle," Charles insulted him. If he'd taken a moment's reflection, he might have been thankful, not only that Diana and the boy were healthy, but that after nine hours of labor, she had given the Windsor dynasty the proverbial "spare," history's insurance in case anything disastrous happened to the first son and heir to the throne.

Or Charles might have considered that baby Henry could someday become the third in a great tradition of *redheaded* English kings of that name: namely, Henry II, patriarch of the Plantagenet dynasty; and England's most notorious Henry, Henry VIII—espouser of six wives, and architect of both the Reformation and the Church of England. Henry's daughters, Mary I and the legendary Elizabeth I, plus their Stuart cousin Mary, Queen of Scots, were famously redheaded as well.

A bit closer to home, Diana's siblings—her older sister Sarah and their brother, Charles, now the 9th Earl Spencer—have russet hair, as do half their ancestors whose portraits grace the walls of Althorp, the family seat, including the ginger-bearded "Red Earl," an antecedent who lived during the reigns of both Victoria and Edward VII.

So what might have spurred the "and he's even got red hair" insult?

Diana, who was deeply unhappy in her marriage, feeling unwelcomed by the royal family and unloved by her adulterous husband, did stray on her own. And throughout Harry's life there have been whispers that his father was not the Prince of Wales, but one of Diana's lovers, the Londonderry-born redhead James Hewitt.

The story for public consumption was that the couple's first encounter took place in the autumn of 1986. By that time, Prince Harry was already two years old. So much for Hewitt's possible paternity. It would not be revealed until later that Hewitt and Diana had first been intimate years earlier than anyone had been led to believe. Perhaps this was enough to plant a seed of doubt in Charles's mind, even though Diana would refer to Harry as "my little Spencer" throughout his childhood.

Little Prince Henry Charles Albert David, henceforth to be known as Harry, as he left the Lindo Wing nestled safely in his mother's arms—Diana wearing a full-sleeved scarlet coat with her golden hair perfectly blown out—was not destined to spend his early childhood in a home filled with marital harmony. When Charles and Diana brought Harry back to their apartments in Kensington Palace, the new dad remained just long enough to down a martini, then dashed off to a previously arranged polo match.

Diana felt abandoned once again.

In the six weeks that had led up to Harry's birth, Diana admitted that she and Charles were very close. But then "suddenly as Harry was born it just went bang, our marriage, the whole thing went down the drain."

That wasn't entirely true, of course.

The royal marriage of Charles and Diana was doomed from the start, and both of them knew it.

CHARLES WAS BORN in November 1948; and when he became "marriageable," it was another era, when royal men were expected to marry virgins, women without a past of any sort, sexual or otherwise—blank slates to be cast in a specific and dutiful royal mold.

In 1978, after Charles's thirtieth birthday came and went and he remained unwed, Prince Philip demanded that his son stop playing the field (or spending time with the married, unsuitable Camilla Parker Bowles) and find an acceptable wife.

The Prince of Wales first met Lady Diana Spencer, the youngest daughter of the 8th Earl Spencer, in 1977 when he was dating her older sister Sarah. Charles recalled Diana as "a very jolly and amusing and attractive sixteen-year-old, full of fun."

Diana remembered "being a fat, podgy, no makeup, unsmart lady, but I made a lot of noise and he liked that."

Over the next few years, the royal family, in a clumsy effort at matchmaking, would begin throwing Charles and Diana together. At a house party in July 1980, the pair found themselves seated side by side on a hay bale. When the naturally sentimental Diana moved to console the prince over the death of Lord Mountbatten—his favorite relative and mentor had been assassinated by an IRA bomb—he began to wonder whether Diana was The One.

Not the one who had won his heart, of course, but the one who could become the perfect Princess of Wales.

Then nineteen-year-old Diana was sweet, naive, and photogenic. Plus, she came from a family that was even more aristocratic and had been in England longer than the Windsors. Above all, she was virginal.

After the couple had enjoyed only thirteen "dates," always in the company of others, on February 24, 1981, Buckingham Palace announced the royal engagement. But there was trouble in paradise from the start. Moments after the announcement, the couple was interviewed by a BBC reporter. In what he surely assumed was a puffball, the journalist asked the duo "And of course in love?"

Wearing a matronly royal blue suit and a white printed blouse with a foulard bow that seemed far too stodgy for a teenager, Diana, standing by her thirty-two-year-old fiancé's side, immediately replied, "Of course."

Charles, however, delivered the first of many emotional blows. He added, "Whatever *love* means."

Boom.

In the days leading up to their marriage, Diana would discover that Charles had never broken off his relationship with Camilla. She often overheard her fiancé cooing to his mistress over the phone. Three weeks before the big day, Diana considered backing out of the royal wedding.

Her sisters Jane and Sarah teased, "Too late, Dutch"—short for *duchess*, Diana's family nickname—"your name's already on the tea towels."

Then, on the eve of her nuptials she discovered a diamond bracelet Charles had purchased for Camilla with the initials *F* and *G*, for Fred and Gladys, their pet names for each other.

But all her life Diana had dreamed of marrying a prince.

She wanted the fairy tale.

She is even on record as having said, "I knew I had to keep myself tidy for what lay ahead."

*Tidy?* What teenager *says* that? One who knew that retaining her virginity was part of the royal protocol.


LIKE CHARLES, DIANA had grown up in an unloving home. But she was a child of divorce.

Diana's mother, born Frances Roche, had an American grandmother. Frances's father, the 4th Baron Fermoy, was the son of New York City socialite Frances Ellen Work, so it's easy to trace Harry's streak of Yankee rebelliousness. Miss Work's family were in the Four Hundred, the social register of New York's most pedigreed residents—a figure that was (falsely) reputed to have corresponded to the exact number of guests who could fit inside society duenna Mrs. Astor's Fifth Avenue ballroom. Miss Work wed the 3rd Baron Fermoy in 1880, during America's Gilded Age when Astors and Vanderbilts and Jeromes looked to unite their fortunes made in stocks and trade to titled English aristocrats on the opposite side of the Atlantic.

In 1967, when Diana was only six, her mother walked out on

the family, deserting her husband, John, and their four young children for Australian wallpaper magnate Peter Shand Kydd. They married two years later.

After his wife abandoned the family, Diana's father Viscount Althorp won custody of their children, but he was often absent as well. In 1975, on the death of his father, he became the 8th Earl Spencer; and the Spencers moved off the Sandringham estate— the royal demesne in Norfolk—to Althorp, the family seat. The following year, he married the divorced Countess of Dartmouth, the former Raine McCorquodale, whom he introduced to his children as a fait accompli.

Diana never bonded with her new stepmother. It was Raine's mother, the prolific Romance novelist Barbara Cartland, who provided Diana with a means of escape from an unloving home. To the outside world, Diana Spencer was a poor little rich girl who seemed to have everything. In truth, her rose-tinted happiness was an illusion similar to the happily ever afters in all the Cartland novels she devoured.

Barely twenty years old when she wed Charles, Diana may have been naive in many respects, one of them believing that he would eventually fall in love with her, as heroes of romance novels do. Yet she was also ambitious. She wanted to be Princess of Wales.

Still, Diana's discovery that Charles was communicating with Camilla even during their shipboard honeymoon aboard the royal yacht *Britannia* sent her into an emotional and psychological tailspin. It was a rocky start to what Diana had hoped would be *her* happily ever after.

After Prince William was born, the couple grew more distant. Diana suffered a miscarriage in 1983. Then Harry was conceived at Sandringham. Diana hoped her pregnancy would repair the multiple fractures in her marriage.

But the princess suffered dreadful morning sickness, as she had when she was carrying William. Diana was convinced by then that her husband had returned to Camilla's arms, and claimed that Harry's conception in itself was a miracle, because by that time her relationship with Charles had become so estranged that they almost never shared the marital four-poster, preferring to sleep apart. Sadly, after Harry was conceived, the Waleses no longer shared a bed at all.

Ken Stronach, who had been Charles's valet for fifteen years and who was disgusted by the prince's long-term adultery with Camilla, confirmed that after Harry's conception, the prince slept on a brass bed in the dressing room of their country house. By then the princess "knew [her husband] had gone back to his lady."

It had not been enough to wound his *wife* with an insult about Harry. At the christening, Prince Charles had the tin-eared temerity to share his disenchantment with Diana's mother, Frances Shand Kydd. "We were so disappointed. We thought it would be a girl."

Frances immediately defended her daughter. "You should realize how lucky you are to have a child that's normal," she retorted, biting Charles's royal head off.

IT'S A SAFE bet that December 21, 1984, was the first and last time Harry was photographed wearing a lacy dress—a 143-year-old christening gown of Honiton lace that was first worn by one of Queen Victoria's daughters, and which every royal baby has been christened in ever since. William was upset when he was told that he could not hold his baby brother, but no one trusted the rambunctious child the family had nicknamed "the basher" with a newborn in a fragile antique. Officiating at Harry's christening in St. George's Chapel at Windsor Castle was Robert Runcie, Archbishop of Canterbury and principal leader of the Church of England. Another royal tradition: the holy water came from the Jordan River.

That day, the merry and not-so-merry wives of Windsor, including one of Harry's godmothers, the Queen's sister Princess Margaret, resembled a floral bouquet, clad in various shades of royal purple and blue with matching hats.

Princess Margaret had been the wild Windsor of her generation, with a legendary, if checkered, romantic history. When she was a teenager, she had fallen in love with her father's equerry, Group Captain Peter Townsend, a man sixteen years her senior. After Townsend's wife divorced him, Margaret and Peter hoped to marry. Theirs was the star-crossed romance of the 1950s. By law, because Margaret was under the age of twenty-five, she required the Queen's consent to marry. But as the monarch is also the head of the Church of England—a church that didn't recognize divorce—Elizabeth was morally obligated to refuse her own sister's request to wed the man she loved. Margaret waited five more years so the matter could go to Parliament; but she ultimately changed her mind about marrying Townsend. One reason might have been their age difference; another might have been that the devoutly religious princess would have been denied a church wedding. Margaret retained her wild streak, however. In 1960, she married a fashion photographer.

WHILE WE THINK of the adult William as the steady, well-behaved one and Harry as the wild child of our era, those personality traits were reversed during their earliest years. Although William was indeed the born organizer, he was also shouting and smashing whatever was in reach, while Harry was, as their mother put it, "more quiet." Still, he was always eager to copy Wills, cheerfully following his lead, beeping the horn of his red tractor as he chased his older brother through the corridors of Craigowan Lodge, their Scottish retreat a mile from the queen's beloved Balmoral, crashing into walls and baseboards with such ferocity that they left a trail of paint chips like freshly fallen snow.

Beloved by sovereigns from Victoria to Elizabeth II, Balmoral is a granite castle built in the Scottish baronial style. To visit is to step back in time. The royal estate itself is situated on 50,000 acres of woodlands—green pine forests, pale birch groves—and rolling parklands. Most of the interior, from the carpeting to the drapes to the upholstery, is tartan. Taxidermy hunting trophies and medieval swords and shields line the walls. Afternoon tea is still poured daily from Queen Victoria's silver teapot, and the royal men dress in kilts, wearing the purple and gray Balmoral tartan; the colors were selected to honor the local flora.

Although Diana missed the urbanity of London and felt suffocated by Balmoral's rusticity and Victorian traditions, her boys adored it. There Prince Philip was the attentive patriarch he had not been for his own son, patiently teaching the young princes to fish the River Dee, known for its salmon; while Charles was the relaxed paternal figure the public never saw, playing hide-and-seek with his sons, taking long walks with them before the morning mist blew off, hiking the rolling moors of purple heather and the rocky granite outcroppings with Harry hoisted on his shoulders. Although Diana was never fond of horses, during their Scottish holidays the young princes learned to become accomplished riders.

In 1980, Charles purchased Highgrove, a 347-acre estate in Gloucestershire, 120 miles from central London; it became his country retreat, with and without Diana. Built in 1796, Highgrove House also happened to be conveniently located just a few miles from Bolehyde Manor, the Wiltshire home of Camilla Parker Bowles, a detail that was not lost on the Princess of Wales. Diana and Charles had separate bedrooms at Highgrove. Hers was filled with cuddly stuffed toys. In Charles's room was a well-loved patched bear that he'd carried everywhere since childhood. Perhaps the Prince of Wales would have become a laughingstock if Fleet Street had revealed this; but to many, this Christopher Robin–hood makes him eminently more relatable.

Harry and William spent most of their weekends at Highgrove, which Charles had transformed into an Edenic paradise, working the farm as well as planting exotic species. Spread across the vast acreage was a meadow carpeted with flowers, lush jungle areas, a stumpery made from tree roots, and box hedges clipped into fantastical topiaries. A pair of sculptured cranes built from recycled auto parts presided over a wild lake. Perhaps coolest of all—to two young boys—was a thatched-roof tree house nestled into a holly tree. Charles was keen to teach his sons the merits of organic farming and had given them pint-size gardening tools; but Harry and William were far more interested in jumping into a giant pool filled with plastic colored balls—where their father would enthusiastically dive in after them—or in playing war games in their tree house, dressed in miniature military fatigues. A frequent visitor to Highgrove was Prince Charles's younger brother Prince Andrew, who had been a helicopter pilot during the Falklands War in 1982. Andrew kept the boys mesmerized with his war stories and piqued their interest in following in his footsteps.

Harry and William had their own nursery (not the botanical variety) with a playroom, sitting room, and bedrooms, where they'd sleep in their striped pajamas, Harry with his thumb in his mouth.

In London, Harry spent his early years in a three-story residence of twenty-eight rooms, Apartments 9 and 10 in the red-brick Kensington Palace, amid 374 acres of landscaped gardens and parkland, most of which is open to the public. There he and William were permitted to treat their home as anything but a palace, racing their BMX bikes around the grounds, brandishing rubber swords as they swashed and buckled through the hallways lined with portraits of centuries-old ancestors, and wood-paneled interiors illuminated by antique chandeliers dripping with crystals. Other famous royal residents of Kensington Palace have included Queen Victoria, who grew up there, as well as Queen Elizabeth's sister, the late Princess Margaret.

Diana had tapped South African interior designer Dudley Poplak to modernize many of the Waleses' rooms in a largely contemporary decor of bright sherbet colors and pastels among the antique furnishings, marble fireplaces, tapestries, and priceless paintings. Their entire top floor was a nursery with professionally stenciled walls, a pair of rocking horses, and a menagerie of stuffed animals. Harry's favorite toy was a Snoopy that had once been Diana's.

Although he would later say that to him she was just Mummy, Harry was born to the most famous, popular, and glamorous woman in the world. Even his father could not compete with Diana for the public's affection. She simply outshone everyone else in the royal family, even the beloved Queen Mother.

Charles, who was clearly jealous of Diana's popularity, would pass it off as a jest during royal walkabouts. "I'm sorry, it's me you've got, not my wife," he'd say with a self-effacing charm that made him his most "human" and likable. It stung that *Diana* was the royal spouse who was the favorite of all the photographers and crowds who clamored for a glimpse of the Waleses—and that it was her face that was plastered all over the newspapers and magazines.

Charles and Diana brought this rivalry, and other sources of tension, home with them. Furious parental rows were the noisy norm. Between 1987 and 1990, when Harry was little more than a toddler, Kensington Palace staff who witnessed his mother's rages described her face as "bright, bright red." The princess would stalk a length of bookcases, punching the volumes as she shouted at Harry's father, "No, Charles, no, I won't, Charles, no, no!" One employee confided that the prince would spew insults at Diana, calling her a "stupid woman" and a "silly young girl."

Even then, the writing was on the wall. "It was awful, I felt so sorry for Diana," said the palace staffer. "It was obvious that the two hated each other and I knew they were bound to separate—I could tell by the way they talked to each other."

The Men in Gray, as Diana referred to the courtiers at Buckingham Palace, were called in to do damage control. What, they pondered, could be causing Diana's bouts of bulimia and sending the Princess of Wales into fits of uncontrollable hysteria? Experts and shrinks were consulted. Drugs were prescribed. But the root cause was abundantly clear: their marriage was damaged beyond repair and Charles was still quite openly carrying on an extramarital affair with the love of his life, Camilla Parker Bowles.

One of the main bones of contention between Charles and Diana was how to bring up their children. Initially, Charles was keen to hire the woman who had been his own nanny to look after the two young princes. Moreover, he favored the royal boys being homeschooled before they were packed off to a string of boarding schools.

It was the way he had been raised. The way it had always been done.

Diana wasn't having any of it. She insisted that her sons be educated as ordinary boys at a regular school. "I want my children to have as normal a life as possible," she insisted. "I want to bring them up with security, not to anticipate things because they will be disappointed." In truth there is nothing normal about being born a son of the House of Windsor and growing up perpetually in the public eye with protection officers from Scotland Yard at their elbow.

But still . . .

Diana's own parents had separated when she was only six years old, and she had endured the pain of feeling abandoned and unloved throughout her life. "I hug my children to death and get into bed with them at night." She said later, "I feed them love and affection. It's so important." So for the first time ever, the heirs to Britain's throne spent their first few years of education in the company of other, nonroyal children.

In 1987, Harry enrolled in a three-year preschool as a "cygnet," the youngest group of students at the tony Mrs. Mynors' Nursery School, on a leafy street called Chepstow Villas, not far from Kensington Palace, where William had been enrolled two years earlier. It was a cheery place where cutouts of balloons decorated the walls. On his first day of school, Harry hadn't wanted to get out of the car; but within a few days, he was scoping out the paparazzi with a set of binoculars made out of a pair of toilet tissue rolls—a true kindergarten project! William had warned Harry not to "trust the 'tographers," so Harry stuck his tongue out at them.

Decades later it was revealed in a documentary that the "'tographers" had provoked the adorable shots by sticking *their* tongues out at the little prince.

At the same age, the boys had also been cautioned to be on their best behavior when they visited their granny the Queen. Naturally, Harry made a goofy face. "And none of that!" Diana would scold.

Aware even during those tender years that William was "special," Harry already felt a bit left out. He would manage to wangle more sick days off from school than William did so that he could have their mummy all to himself. Diana was not unaware of his machinations, and her heart ached for the little boy who so resembled her elder sister Sarah.

There were occasions when the Waleses were a normalish family of four. In happier times, on days when the couple had no formal engagements, sometimes Diana would pick up the boys at school and then stop at the local Sainsbury's grocery store for candy or at the video store, where Harry would select—what else?—action flicks. The princess would spend the rest of the afternoon catching some rays in the garden at *KP*—as Kensington Palace is colloquially known—while the princes romped on the playground equipment and Charles played grill master, barbecuing foil-wrapped potatoes and salmon for dinner.

Other days, after school Diana would take Harry and William shopping along Kensington High Street, part of her campaign to provide them with a more assimilated upbringing. With the Princess of Wales disguised in a dark wig and sunglasses, to the immense amusement of her sons, Harry browsed for his favorite action hero comic books among the shelves of WHSmith. They indulged in fast food from McDonald's. Diana took them sightseeing to the sort of tourist attractions that would excite little boys, including the zoo and the dungeon. They rode the Tube, went go-karting, and patronized local cinemas. Diana gave the princes pocket change for their purchases so they could learn the value of money. Charles never gave them money and never understood why they needed it. Royals traditionally didn't carry money; if Harry and William wanted something, they could just ask their protection officers to buy it for them. The princes also queued up like civilian children to sit on Father Christmas's ample lap at Selfridges department store.

But while the "normal" kids in the queue might have begged Santa Claus for a train set, *Harry's* was a gift from the London Underground itself.

The Waleses' divergent views on child rearing were just one example of the increasing emotional distance between them, but they often lived separate lives as well. In May 1988, when Harry was only three and a half years old, he was rushed to Great Ormond Street Hospital, where an emergency hernia operation was performed. Charles was en route to Italy at the time, headed for a painting holiday; Camilla was allegedly accompanying him. When Charles reached Paris and was informed of Harry's medical emergency, he offered to fly right home. He checked in on

Harry's condition every half hour by phone and was assured by Diana that it wasn't necessary. Harry was swiftly out of danger and there was no need for him to return to London. The princess spent the night sleeping in a chair by Harry's hospital bed. The story the press ran with was that of a golden-haired Madonna mother and an indifferent absentee father.

In September 1989, when Harry turned five, he once again followed in William's footsteps and entered Wetherby Preparatory School in Notting Hill, not far from where he had attended Mrs. Mynors'.

Despite their attending school with nonroyal children, the princes knew they were different. At the age of six, Harry lorded it over eight-year-old William, saying, "You'll be king, I won't, so I can do what I want!"

It was at Wetherby where Harry first made good on this royal proclamation. He was a bratty prankster, literally pulling the trouser leg of music master Robert Pritchard. Harry's protection officer Ken Wharfe tried to discipline his pint-size charge. "Shut up, Harry."

Finally, when the instructor could stand the prince's pestering no longer, he said, "What is it, Harry?"

The imp indicated the teacher's open fly and replied, "I can see your willy, Mr. Pritchard!"

Diana was hysterical with laughter when she learned about the incident. Two days later, when she was back at Wetherby, she approached the hapless music teacher and said, "Mr. Pritchard, I hear my son saw your willy the other day."

No wonder Diana once said, "Harry's like me. He's the naughty one."

With Diana playing "good cop" and Charles frequently on official duties, the nanny was often charged with disciplining Harry.

By 1990, both spouses were leaking stories to the press. Staff were expected to choose sides.

Nanny Jessie Webb was a no-nonsense Cockney who assessed the situation quickly. "Those boys are going to need a lot of help if they're not going to end up as barking mad as their dad and mum." According to Harry's biographer Marcia Moody, Webb's first royal job "didn't get off to a good start." As Moody puts it, according to Harry's protection officer Ken Wharfe, "Jessie was an interesting character . . . a good nanny, but more of a fun person." The princes "used to play Jessie up because she wasn't really their type." Because Harry could indeed be a handful at times, Nanny Webb would, confided Wharfe, "come and knock on my door and say, 'Ken, can you have a word with them, they're being very naughty.'" And then the protection officer would be the one to give Harry a talking-to, reminding the prince that he had to listen to Jessie.

"I don't like her," Harry protested.

"Well, you'd better get to like her. I gather you've been rude to her. What did you say?"

"I told her she should lose weight."

"Well, that's not very nice, Harry, is it?"

Ultimately Diana managed to coax an apology from her son—always a teachable moment in kindness, empathy, and compassion.

It was hard for anyone to remain cross with Harry for long. He was a lovable, huggable little boy. Wharfe described him as "a friendly Labrador dog who liked everybody." And he was always up for treats. "If someone took him off and gave him some food, he would go."

BECAUSE WILLIAM OFTEN received special attention given his status as firstborn, Diana was keenly aware that Harry often felt left out. Harry had displayed an early interest in firearms and all things military, so Diana used her influence to secure visits to such facilities as the Metropolitan Police Firearms Training Centre in Lippitts Hill; and when Harry was about seven or eight years old, a boyhood dream came true: he was permitted to shoot a gun. He discovered he was good at it. Harry had found his calling—one he never grew out of.

Harry's interest in the army from an early age is also credited in part to James Hewitt, the princes' equestrian instructor (and considerably more to their mother). Hewitt was an officer in the Life Guards, the senior regiment of the British army and part of the Household Cavalry, the security unit that protects the royal family. Hewitt enthralled Harry and William with his war stories and had miniature camouflage uniforms made for them. Hewitt also used his army contacts to show Harry and William the high-tech military equipment at the army camps in Wiltshire. Diana made sure that her sons were appropriately appreciative and wrote thank-you notes to Hewitt after each visit to a training camp.

Just days after his eighth birthday in September 1992, after a shaky start, Harry found his footing at the exclusive Ludgrove School, set on 130 acres of rolling Berkshire countryside. Ludgrove was home to two hundred boys from ages eight to thirteen, one of whom was his older brother. Harry may have looked angelic in his school uniform of corduroy pants and tweed jacket, but his behavior was positively devilish. At Ludgrove, Harry became both a daredevil and the class clown, demonstrating a rebellious streak that—for better or worse (and sometimes both)—made him the "bad boy" of the present-day Windsors, a reputation of his own making that has followed him all his life.

As their parents' marriage continued to deteriorate, William, now older and more aware of their perpetual tensions, became quieter and more sensitive, while Harry got into all manner of mischief. He dared a quartet of boys to moon the paparazzi who lay in wait for him behind a hedge on the school's footpath, and aimed pillows at his dorm mates with such accuracy that they would fall out of bed. Harry also sparked a schoolwide alert when he lost his GPS security tag. He was supposed to wear it at all times so that his Scotland Yard protection officers knew where he was. Panic ensued when it went missing. The tag was eventually located in Harry's laundry bag.

Yet everyone at Ludgrove seemed to have the ginger prince's back. William had helped Harry settle in, and the house matron permitted him to watch *Star Trek*, with a cup of hot cocoa. Not one to abuse his privilege, Harry soon convinced the matron to permit the other boys in his dorm to join him in front of the telly.

The headmaster, Gerald Barber, and his wife also took care to ensure that Ludgrove was a safe haven for Harry and William, banning newspapers from the school in order to shield the princes from the daily deluge of headlines detailing their parents' ongoing feud. The media were not permitted on the school's verdant manicured grounds. Photographers had no access to the property, except for a footpath that ran between the ball fields and the school.

Unfortunately, when Harry and William went home to Kensington Palace on weekends, they saw what was being written about their mum and dad because Diana did read the tabloids. The emotional health of two little boys was of no concern to the demon barons of Fleet Street, who were only interested in selling papers.

Harry had been at Ludgrove for three months when their mother made the hour-long drive to the school to inform both him and William that she and their papa were separating: they just couldn't live together anymore. As they sat in the headmaster's living room, Diana was quick to reassure the boys that nothing in their lives would change. They would still reside in Kensington Palace. Weekends would still be spent at Highgrove. Harry burst into tears.

Yet Harry's biographer Marcia Moody provides another account of this incident. She states that Ken Wharfe had asked Diana how her talk with the princes went and she told him that the boys had been generally unperturbed by the news; and that afterward, they had requested permission to go out and play.

If this account is the accurate one, perhaps they were in shock and needed time to process such immense news, even though their mum had just told them that life would go on as before. Perhaps Harry and William had been well enough insulated from the worst by the Barbers. Perhaps they were too young to take it all in. Perhaps Harry was more focused on his struggles with Ludgrove's academics—his bugaboo all throughout his training of any kind. He always excelled at sports and extracurriculars, and his leadership skills were commendable. But according to Harry's biographer Duncan Larcombe, he suffers from mild dyslexia—which would put him in the good company of other famous dyslexics like Leonardo da Vinci, Albert Einstein, Walt Disney, and Harry's friend Virgin entrepreneur Richard Branson.

On November 24, 1992, the Queen gave a speech at London's Guildhall, to mark the fortieth anniversary of her accession, in which she referred to 1992 as an *annus horribilis*—a horrible year. It certainly had been a nightmare for the royal family.

In January, Harry's uncle and aunt, Andrew and "Fergie"—the Duke and Duchess of York—split, following photos of Sarah cavorting on the French Riviera with Texas oil baron Steve Wyatt. But those images weren't nearly as shocking as the tabloid snaps of Fergie sunbathing topless while her "financial advisor" John Bryan sucked on her toes.

That spring, *Diana: Her True Story* was published. Diana had secretly collaborated on the book with Dr. James Coldhurst and journalist Andrew Morton. This confessional, warts-and-all version of her life as Princess of Wales shattered the fairy-tale story line that had been scripted for her, and named Camilla as the reason for the breakup of her marriage.

In August, Harry, William, and the rest of the world learned that Diana had been unfaithful to Charles in the scandal that was to become known as Squidgygate. The news broke of an illegally taped phone call between the Princess of Wales and her lover James Gilbey, a Lotus car dealer and the heir to the gin fortune of the same name. During the lengthy telephone conversation Gilbey called Diana *darling*, as well as Squidge and Squidgy, several times. From the substance of the conversation, it was obvious that they were more than just good friends. Perhaps even more damning, Diana was heard on the tape venting about specific members of the royal family, particularly Charles, who she complained to Gilbey "makes my life real torture."

In November, Charles and Diana made their final official visit together as a couple. It was clear they couldn't stand each other, and *that* became the news story. Diana had to break it to their sons.

Later that month, on November 20, the Queen's forty-fifth wedding anniversary, fire engulfed her beloved Windsor Castle, destroying the roof and a major part of the State Apartments. The monarch was met with a massive public backlash when she initially sought taxpayer reimbursement for the restoration, because Windsor Castle is a private royal residence and was not open to the public as a sightseeing destination at the time. The £36.5 million price tag for the restoration was eventually resolved by the royal family's concession to charge the public an entry fee for castle precincts and to open Buckingham Palace to the public, with an £8 admission price for the next five years. The Queen not only contributed £2 million of her own money but also agreed to start paying income tax beginning in 1993, the first British monarch to do so since the 1930s.

CHARLES WAS CONCERNED about the effect the perpetual marital squabbles were having on Harry and William. "I want them to remember that I was not the one doing all the shouting and screaming," he confided to a former girlfriend, Janet Jenkins. One does not have to remain emotionless and aloof to be blameless, obviously; and Diana had good reason to lose her temper, if not her mind. Charles had a warm pair of arms waiting for him elsewhere.

Incensed over Diana's "incessant game playing" (pot, meet kettle), Charles was the one who demanded a legal separation.

On December 9, 1992, from the floor of the House of Commons, Prime Minister John Major announced the formal separation of the Prince and Princess of Wales. His remarks had been written by Her Majesty's senior staff. Major announced that the decision had "been reached amicably and [Charles and Diana] will both continue to participate fully in the upbringing of their children" (which they did, in separate establishments). Major's statement continued: "They believe that a degree of privacy and understanding is essential if Their Royal Highnesses are to provide a happy and secure upbringing for their children."

The hacked, compromising Squidgygate telephone conversation had actually taken place in December 1989, even though the transcripts were not sold to the press until 1992. Diana's popularity plummeted after the revelation.

But if Squidgygate was an embarrassment to the royal family, especially to Diana's sons, what must they have thought when in January 1993, Camillagate once and for all revealed their father's adultery with Camilla Parker Bowles?

Like the call between Diana and James Gilbey, the nocturnal conversation between Charles and Camilla also took place in December 1989. It may have been a composite of more than one phone call. However, when the tapes were played and the full transcript published, it wasn't so much Charles's desire to get into Camilla's knickers that set tongues wagging; but the manner in which he wished to do it—as one of her tampons. This was just too much for everyone, especially the Queen.

The Christmas holiday of 1992 was the first that Harry had not shared with his mother. The royal family traditionally spends Christmas at Sandringham, and it was imperative that the princes enjoy the holiday there with their father. After the warring Waleses formally separated, Diana was no longer welcome there. The princess missed her boys, but not the de rigueur Boxing Day bird shoot. "They're always shooting things," she remarked in disgust, having never been a fan of the outdoorsy pastimes that the Windsors take so seriously.

From then on, for the next few years, Harry and William enjoyed the best of both worlds with their parents, who would endeavor to outdo each other to take them on ever more glamorous vacations. Diana took the princes on summer holidays to the Caribbean and Disneyland. With their papa they skied at Klosters and spent quality time at Balmoral with their grandparents.

During those frosty winter months of 1993, the Waleses' personal possessions were legally divided. Charles moved out of Kensington Palace and into York House, which had been constructed on the remains of a hospital for female lepers, and which was the official residence of the monarch before Buckingham Palace was built. He had Highgrove professionally redecorated, transforming the rooms into a neo-Edwardian man cave, erasing all traces of Diana. There wasn't even a photograph of her with their boys. Diana, who had begun to consult astrologers, psychic healers, and New Age gurus, had the KP apartments "smudged" to smoke out the bad juju. Her renovation consisted of an influx of modern art into a decor of pastels, white lace, and candles. She did retain a few photos of Charles; after all, he was the father of their children. About the only things she and Charles had in common now were Harry, William, and a penchant for organic food.

But there was much more to Diana than woo-woo and gurus. The princess was passionate about helping the poorest and most disadvantaged people and directly involved her sons, engaging them in ways they would never forget. She traveled with the Red Cross to Zimbabwe in order to focus awareness on the plight of refugees. She visited a leprosy hospital in Kathmandu. Another of her charities was Centrepoint, which provides support and shelter to London's at-risk youth. Diana frequently visited Centrepoint with William and Harry, where they played cards and chatted with the residents.

Charles hired a new nanny for the boys, the stunning, sporty, Alexandra "Tiggy" Legge-Bourke. Although Tiggy hailed from an aristocratic family, she was also a boisterous tomboy who was a crack shot, could gut a stag, and skin a rabbit. Tiggy, a close friend of Charles's, had previously run a London nursery school called Miss Tiggywinkle's; and her mother had been a lady-in-waiting to Charles's sister, the Princess Royal.

To their mother's dismay, both Harry and William immediately took to Tiggy, who seemed more like another indulgent playmate than a stern governess. In Diana's sorrow over the marital separation, she feared she was losing her boys' affection to this interloper, and also (incorrectly) suspected that Tiggy had supplanted her in Charles's bed. Diana didn't take kindly to Tiggy's referring to the princes as "my babies," or that Tiggy smoked in front of them (both boys would take up smoking in their teens). But Tiggy was no pushover and defended herself. "I give them what they need at this age—fresh air, a rifle, and a horse. She gives them a tennis racquet and a bucket of popcorn at the movies."

During the next two years, although William tried to shield his brother from the revelations of their parents' infidelities, Harry grew up faster than any child, even one who lives in a metaphorical fishbowl, should have to do. To their immense credit, the princes never turned against either of their parents. They were raised not only with a keen sense of duty, but to suppress their emotions and carry on.

Harry was only nine in July 1994, when his father was interviewed for ITV by Jonathan Dimbleby for the documentary *Charles: The Private Man, The Public Role*. For the first time, the Prince of Wales openly confessed to his adulterous affair with Camilla, insisting that he had really endeavored to be faithful to his marriage vows with Diana, "until it became irretrievably broken down, us both having tried."

Harry was stunned. During a previous debate about the future of the monarchy, when the name of his father's mistress was raised, the prince had innocently asked, "Who's Camilla?" and was promptly ushered upstairs. Now the puzzle pieces were falling into place.

The day after the interview aired, media pundits questioned Charles's suitability to succeed his mother on the throne. NOT FIT TO REIGN, screamed the headline of the tabloid *Daily Mirror*. Shortly thereafter, the biography of Charles titled *The Prince of Wales: An Intimate Portrait* was published. In the wake of its release Andrew Parker Bowles divorced his wife and married his own longtime girlfriend.

Then author Anna Pasternak published a tell-all, *Princess in Love*, in which James Hewitt purported to spill the beans on his affair with Harry's mother, proving that Diana could not claim the high road over Charles when it came to fidelity. Diana had also been romantically linked to other men, some of them married. There were even humiliating leaks of harassing phone calls she'd made to various paramours.

Diana was just desperate to be loved. Her parents had rejected her. Her husband had rejected her. Cruelest of all—but to their sons as well—was Charles's admission in the pages of *The Prince of Wales: A Biography* that his father had forced him into marrying Diana and that he had never loved her.

"Whatever *love* is," indeed.

Diana took revenge in November 1995, in an interview that was televised on Charles's forty-seventh birthday. On the *Pan-*

*orama* broadcast with Martin Bashir, she stated that she believed Charles was unworthy of the crown and not suited to be king. The Princess of Wales claimed that her husband was the first to stray, and that Camilla had remained in the picture throughout their marriage. In her soft, aristocratic voice, Diana looked up from uncharacteristically black-rimmed and heavily mascaraed eyes and fired a shot heard round the world. She told Martin Bashir, "There were three of us in this marriage, so it was a bit crowded."

It was the first time that Harry, who was watching the broadcast from the living room of one of his Ludgrove history teachers, had heard about his mother's extramarital relationship with James Hewitt and her battle with bulimia. Before that night, Harry had assumed Hewitt was merely his riding instructor and a mentor: a guy who encouraged his interest in all things military and bought him pint-size camo uniforms when he was younger. Diana had always been appalled by the insidious rumors speculating that Hewitt was actually Harry's father; and while that was untrue, she did admit Hewitt had been her lover.

The Queen had seen too much dirty linen about the royal family aired in the media, and Diana's *Panorama* interview was the final straw. Toward the end of 1995, the monarch wrote to Charles and Diana individually, insisting they divorce.

LONG BEFORE THE divorce decree came down, Diana had announced that she was retiring from public life—but ultimately she could never cease her tireless charitable and philanthropic efforts. This, in addition to her boys, were what was dearest to her heart, what made the spotlight worth the dark side of celebrity.

Harry was only nine years old when Diana brought him and William to Passage, a homeless shelter near London's Vauxhall Bridge, so they could see that just a few miles from where they dwelled in splendor and comfort at Kensington Palace, others were desperately in need.

Diana also called attention to other issues that many at the time shunned as too frightening. She hugged AIDS patients. She campaigned to remove land mines from conflict zones, so there would be no more collateral damage to innocent children. Diana had compassion for children everywhere; and Harry too would ultimately embrace his mother's lessons, developing the same easy relationship with, and love for, kids.

On August 28, 1996, a little more than two weeks before Harry's twelfth birthday, the divorce decree, called a *decree nisi* in England, was stamped. Diana would receive a settlement of £17 million. Harry's parents being legally divorced was a rarity in the royal family at the time—although it would become an all-too-common event among the offspring of Elizabeth II, with three of her four children ultimately ending their first marriages. Princess Margaret's marriage to photographer Anthony Armstrong-Jones had also ended in divorce. But well into the twentieth century, divorced persons were considered such societal pariahs that they were not even welcome at court or permitted in the royal box at Ascot. Diana was also being formally stripped of her title as a Royal Highness. Harry and William's mother would henceforth be styled simply as Diana, Princess of Wales. Retaining her royal title was important in terms of Diana's social status and ability to raise funds for the comprehensive charity work and philanthropy that had become her raison d'être. Upset by the indignity, Prince William assured his mum that he would restore her HRH when he became king.

Sadly, he would never be able to fulfill his promise.

# Hollywood Royalty

On July 29, 1981, a heavily pregnant Doria Loyce Ragland and her husband, Thomas Markle, were among the estimated global audience of 750 million people who were glued to their television sets to watch the royal wedding of the Prince of Wales to Lady Diana Spencer.

How could Doria and Thomas ever have imagined that the second son born to the couple they were witnessing tie the knot would someday get down on one knee and offer a diamond ring to the daughter in Doria's belly? Americans have better odds of winning the lottery.

Six days after Diana became Princess of Wales, on August 4, 1981, Rachel Meghan Markle was born in Los Angeles, California. She inherited her wavy brown hair, freckles, and seductive dark eyes from her African American mother and the quirky kink at the tip of her nose from her Caucasian father.

Meghan's parents had a true Hollywood marriage, however; "meeting cute," as the expression goes. In the late 1970s, Thomas Markle, a divorced father of two, was a lighting director for the popular ABC soap opera *General Hospital* at the Columbia/Sunset Gower Studios when he fell for Doria Ragland, who was temping as an assistant makeup artist. "I think he was drawn to her sweet eyes and her Afro, plus their shared love of antiques," Meghan would later write in an essay for *Elle UK* magazine about growing up biracial. Thomas, then thirty-five, and Doria, twenty-three, married on December 23, 1979, at the New Agey Self-Realization Fellowship Temple on Sunset Boulevard. The six-foot-three-inch groom, wearing a tweed blazer and ginger-hued shirt, towered over his five-foot-two-inch bride. Doria looked like a schoolgirl in a modest white pleated skirt and short-sleeved blouse, with a coronet of baby's breath in her hair. Their only child was born less than two years later.

From the start, Meghan was adored in equal measure by both her parents. Doria's nickname for her has always been Flower. According to his son from his first marriage, Thomas Jr., who moved back in with his father and stepmother when he was fourteen, Thomas Markle had been a workaholic—until Meghan was born. "Dad's work took priority over everything, but she became his whole world. I remember when she came home from the hospital he had decorated the bathroom with little angels and fairies. He would keep holding her up to the mirror so she could see herself in his arms. The look on his face was priceless."

From the time she was a baby, it seemed pretty clear that Meghan was a "daddy's girl."

Her half brother said, "Dad would take so many pictures of Meggie that she must have been the most photographed baby in the San Fernando Valley. He must have about fifty thousand pictures of her stashed away somewhere. Meggie was a little princess long before she met Harry. She was her daddy's princess."

The family lived in a neighborhood that Meghan described as "leafy and affordable." On paper, a great place to raise their daughter. What the area wasn't, was diverse. "There was my mom, caramel in complexion, with her light-skinned baby in tow, being asked where my mother was, since they assumed she was my nanny."

Meghan acknowledges that she was too young at the time to

comprehend how difficult it must have been for her parents to endure such institutional prejudice—"what the world was like for them"—but they made it a safe and happy place for her.

When Meghan was about seven years old, she coveted a particular boxed set of Barbie dolls for Christmas. The Heart Family consisted of a mommy, a daddy, and two kids. The perfect nuclear family, according to Mattel. But the sets were sold only in white families or black families. Meghan recalls not particularly caring at the time which set she received—just that she wanted one of them. In her immediate family, skin color had never been politicized. One day, her mother picked her up from her grandmother's house, and "there were the three of us, a family tree in an ombre of mocha next to the caramel complexion of my mom and light-skinned, freckled me. I remember having the sense of belonging, having nothing to do with the color of my skin."

That Christmas morning, under the tree was a box wrapped in holiday paper flecked with glitter. Meghan unwrapped her gift to discover a black mommy, a white daddy, and a child of each skin color. Her father had customized the Heart Family for her.

Thomas Markle had grown up in a small blue-collar town in Pennsylvania. In the late eighteenth century his ancestor Johann Markel picked up stakes in his hometown of Offenburg, which was located directly across the Rhine from Strasbourg in the German region of Baden-Württemberg. Johann emigrated to America, settling in Pennsylvania, home to countless German immigrants of the day—hence the term Pennsylvania Dutch, given to those who spoke their native language, *Deutsch*, or German, after their arrival in that part of America.

Johann's double-great-grandson Isaac—Thomas Markle's great-grandfather—was a laborer in a lumber mill there. It was a hard life. Isaac's ancestors died of pneumonia and cirrhosis of the liver. Meghan's paternal grandfather Gordon, a veteran of World War II, worked on the railroads. The alteration in the spelling of their surname from Markel to Markle was purportedly due to an error made by a census taker.

Doris, Meghan's grandmother and the family matriarch, worked at the local five-and-dime. The Markles were God-fearing and upwardly mobile. After leaving school, Thomas had a job at the local bowling alley as a pinsetter, but that was never how he envisioned spending the rest of his life. His ambition was to be a stage technician. At the age of twenty, he moved to Chicago, where he worked on local theater and television productions, keeping his color blindness a secret from his bosses—one he transcended, eventually becoming an award-winning Hollywood lighting designer.

Thomas was only twenty when he met a pretty redhead named Roslyn Loveless. She was already pregnant with Samantha, the first of their two children, when they married. Samantha's brother, Thomas Jr., was born two years later. Embracing the free and easy hippie lifestyle of the 1960s, the first Markle family lived in the Chicago suburb of Hyde Park, tootling around in a battered blue VW van. But according to a family friend, Thomas hadn't really been ready to settle down with a wife and kids. Within eight years the marriage was over. Roslyn moved to New Mexico with their children while Thomas headed for that iconic Hollywood sign. In the Los Angeles sunshine, he partied as hard as he worked.

Cut to 1979, when Doria Ragland stepped into his life. Superimpose a heart around their close-up.

Fade and dissolve to Great Britain during the Middle Ages. Madrigal music underscores our journey into the past.

Whenever anyone marries into the British royal family, especially if the bride is a commoner from a nonaristocratic family, genealogists have a field day. For example, just prior to their wedding, Catherine Middleton and Prince William were discovered to be fourteenth cousins once removed through his mother and fifteenth cousins through his father. Their common ancestors go all the way back to the Plantagenets and the reign of Edward III, who ruled for fifty years, from 1327 to 1377.

Kate and the beloved late Queen Mother share an ancestor as well. Australian art historian Michael Reed, who discovered the link when researching the provenance of a famous antique cabinet in the collection of New York's Metropolitan Museum of Art, said that it made sense for Kate to wear the Queen Mother's scroll tiara when she married Prince William. "Both women share a great deal: Durham ancestry, the vast Gibside Estate, and the same famous cabinet." Reed's research revealed that the Blakiston Baronets and the Baronets of Conyers of Horden, Kate's ancestors, were the wealthiest landowners in Northern England. They married into the Bowes-Lyon family so that they could share each other's vast coal estates at Gibside. Kate's direct ancestor, Sir Thomas Blakiston Conyers, also attended the funeral of his Gibside cousin Mary Bowes, Countess of Strathmore and Kinghorne. Mary was the Queen Mother's triple-great-grandmother, who at the time of her death in 1800 was thought to be the wealthiest woman in England.

According to genealogist Gary Boyd Roberts, a researcher at the New England Historic Genealogical Society in Boston, Meghan and Harry are seventeenth cousins, thanks again to the prolific Edward III, who had nine children. According to Roberts, one of Edward's myriad descendants was an ancestor of Meghan's father, Reverend William Skipper, who arrived in New England in 1639—a mere nineteen years after the *Mayflower* disgorged its passengers in Plymouth.

Their other common ancestors can be traced back to the fifteenth century: Sir Philip Wentworth, a knight and courtier who was the great-grandfather of Jane Seymour, third queen of Henry VIII; Mary Clifford, daughter of John Clifford, the 7th Baron de Clifford; and Elizabeth Bowes and her husband, Richard Bowes, son of Sir Ralph Bowes of Streatlam Castle and High Sheriff of

County Durham, born in 1480—ancestors of Queen Elizabeth, the Queen Mother (née Bowes-Lyon).

Although it's a bit of a stretch, it's possible that Meghan Markle's roots, like Kate Middleton's, might also be traced to Britain's coal mines. Meghan's double-great paternal grandmother Martha Sykes, who was born in a coal-mining region of Yorkshire, emigrated to America with her parents Thomas and Mary in 1869, during the reign of Queen Victoria. Their names are found in the 1870 census from the Mahanoy Township in Schuylkill County, a mining area of Pennsylvania, when Martha was just three years old. The family, which would eventually swell to five children, would have dwelled in a rough-hewn lumber shack with no indoor plumbing. Open sewers outside would have been magnets for disease. Thomas Sykes, who toiled as a collier, unfortunately did not achieve the better life he'd dreamt of when he left his homeland. Just eight years after his arrival on American soil, he died at the age of forty-three, leaving Mary a widow with five children.

Martha Sykes survived her Dickensian childhood to marry into the Markle family. Her great-grandson Thomas is Meghan's father, who grew up poor in Pennsylvania.

Back on British soil, further digging into the roots of Meghan's family tree reveals a slightly unpleasant hiccup, as the British might say. But it occurred ten generations ago, when Meghan's ancestor Lord Hussey, 1st Baron Hussey of Sleaford, orchestrated a rather ill-advised plot to overthrow Prince Harry's ancestor, King Henry VIII. As every schoolchild knows, Henry was fond of beheading people who crossed him. Such was the fate of Lord Hussey, whose lands, as well as his head, became forfeit to the crown.

Hussey met a bad end, but his great-great-grandchild, yet another adventurous seafarer in Meghan's genealogy, Captain Christopher Hussey, sailed from England in the 1650s and became one of the founding fathers of the island of Nantucket. Another descendant of Lord Hussey—and an ancestor of Meghan's—is Mary Hussey Smith, who became a major landowner in nineteenth-century New Hampshire.

It's also possible that Meghan may not be the first of her family to enter the hallowed halls of Windsor Castle, although she will certainly be the first to do so as a duchess rather than as a domestic. Family lore via a second cousin of Meghan's father, former U.S. Air Force colonel Ken Barbi, holds that Markle's triple-great-grandmother Mary Bird worked at the palaces. A search of royal household staff records did locate an M. Bird who was employed at Windsor Castle in 1856.

Whether she had an ancestor who polished the royal silver or not, what is undeniable, however, is that Meghan Markle will be the first person to marry into the British royal family who is a descendant of slaves.

During the same years Mary Bird may or may not have been working for Queen Victoria, and while other Markle ancestors were living in prosperity in New England, the other side of Meghan's family were forced to live as someone's *property* in rural Georgia.

A run-down railway town almost due south of Atlanta, Jonesboro has some unusual claims to fame. The site of a Civil War battle, it was also where the author of *Gone With the Wind*, Margaret Mitchell, spent a good deal of her childhood.

Richard Ragland was born into slavery near Jonesboro in 1830. That part of Georgia, Clayton County, was on the edge of the frontier. Revolutionary War veterans were encouraged to become pioneers by entering lotteries where they could win land. But it was rough, inhospitable territory, recently seized by white men from Native Americans—nothing of the moonlight and magnolias of Mitchell's revisionist fantasy. For those who had the misfortune to live there, Jonesboro was a hardscrabble existence; even the local landowners were looked down on by Georgia's coastal cotton barons.

One of the veterans who settled this hostile land was an American of English descent who had fought for the fledgling nation against the crown. William Ragland was a Methodist who emigrated from Cornwall. A planter and land speculator, he had moved from Virginia to North Carolina, then seized the opportunity to head south to Georgia with his slaves. Slaves were often given their masters' surnames, and Meghan's ancestor was owned by William Ragland. After his emancipation, Richard and his descendants became one of Georgia's black families named Ragland. Richard's son Steve married a white woman. If Meghan's parents were looked at askance in the Southern California of the 1980s, imagine how people in rural Georgia of the Reconstruction era regarded Steve Ragland and his wife, Texie Hendrick!

Successive generations of the Ragland family, black, white, and mixed race, toiled primarily in menial jobs—factory workers, domestics, and janitors—in America's Deep South. Meghan's great-great-grandparents, Jeremiah Ragland and Claudie Ritchie, both recorded in a census as "mulatto," managed to get out of Jonesboro, moving to Chattanooga, Tennessee, where Claudie was a maid in a shop. Jeremiah was a saloon porter, but he also acquired the skills to work in various trades, first as a barber, and later setting up his own shop as a tailor. Time marched on. And with it came better opportunities.

Fleeing the region's prejudice and violence during the Jim Crow era, the family moved north, then west, part of the Great Migration that dates to the First World War. With so many white men being sent overseas to fight, the recruitment of African Americans by northern industries resulted in employment opportunities. The reasons for leaving the South were aspirational as well. There were simply more possibilities for a better life.

On Meghan's maternal grandmother's side, her ancestors

Hunter and Gertrude migrated to Ohio with their daughter Nettie. On her maternal grandfather's side, Meghan's great-aunt Dora became a teacher. Dora's nephew Alvin—Meghan's maternal grandfather—was an antiques dealer who collected vintage cars. In 1940, Alvin was an unemployed former gas station attendant when he registered for the draft.

In California, the Raglands became teachers and Realtors, the family's first white-collar jobs.

Alvin married Nettie's daughter Jeanette, a nurse who gave birth in 1956 to Meghan's mother, Doria.

When Doria was seven years old, her parents took a car trip from Ohio to California with their three kids.

Meghan was eleven when her maternal grandparents told her the story of that journey. Years later, in her thirties, she wrote about their experience on her lifestyle blog, The Tig, in a Martin Luther King Day post on January 9, 2015.

When Meghan was a child, road trips meant "Are we there yet?"

*Things were different then*, her grandfather Alvin told her.

"Meggie, on our road trip, when we went to Kentucky Fried Chicken, we had to go to the back for 'coloreds.' The kitchen staff handed me the chicken from the back door and we ate in the parking lot. That's just what it was."

*That's just what it was.*

Years after she first heard her grandparents' anecdote about their experience in the Jim Crow South, Meghan remained haunted by it. She wrote: "It reminds me of how young our country is. How far we've come and how far we still have to come. It makes me think of the countless black jokes people have shared in front of me, not realizing I am mixed. Unaware that I am the ethnically ambiguous fly on the wall. It makes me wonder what my parents experienced as a mixed race couple."

Meghan closed her blog post with a dedication that quoted Dr. King: to her "mom and dad for choosing each other 'not for the color of their skin but for the content of their character' . . . to all of you champions of change: *Thank you.*"

Meghan's grandparents eventually divorced, and Alvin married Ava Burrows, now a retired teacher. Ms. Burrows is totally tickled by her step-granddaughter's impending marriage, telling an interviewer, "Meggie marrying a prince? Who'd have thunk!" She slapped her thigh in amusement. "I'm kind of expecting a visit from the men in black suits [the FBI] to check us out. I guess it's like your Downtown [*sic*] Abbey—and we're the folks downstairs."

Meghan's mother, Doria Ragland, whom Meghan describes as a "free spirit," is said to be as effervescent as her daughter. "Giggly, warm, passionate, brilliant, nurturing, and fun," according to a friend who has known her since Meghan was a baby.

Doria was born and raised in a middle-class African American community of Los Angeles. In middle age, she earned a master's degree in social work from the University of Southern California and became a certified yoga instructor. Her specialty is working with geriatric clients. Doria still lives in Los Angeles, in View Park–Windsor Hills, one of the wealthiest primarily African American residential neighborhoods in the United States. If a romance novelist wrote that Meghan Markle headed from View Park–Windsor Hills to Windsor Castle, her editor would likely request her to change the name of the neighborhood because it sounds too perfectly pat to actually be true!

Meghan's parents separated when she was only two years old, but they made every attempt to provide their young daughter with a stable home environment. After the separation, the three of them would still vacation together. On Sunday evenings, after Meghan spent weekends with her father, the burly, bearded Thomas would drop her back at her mother's apartment, a second-story flat situated above a garage in the ethnically diverse Miracle Mile neighborhood on a wide street lined with stately royal palms.

The single-family homes and low-rise multiunit dwellings have the classic Southern California architecture: stucco facades with red-tile roofs. Out front, postage-stamp-sized lawns are fringed with flowers and succulents. Upstairs, in Doria's apartment, after Thomas brought Meghan home, the trio would watch *Jeopardy!* together as they ate their dinner off TV trays in front of the set. "We were still so close-knit," Meghan recalls.

Never once did little Meghan see her parents arguing. Nevertheless, in 1987, when she was only six years old, her parents finally divorced, citing irreconcilable differences. They were awarded joint custody of Meghan, with the agreement that she would reside mainly with her mother and spend some weeks as well as some summer holidays with her father—similar to Prince Harry's situation after his parents separated. Although Meghan lived with her mother, she was extremely close to her father as well. She often saw her half-siblings when she visited her dad, and got along well with Thomas Jr., fifteen years her senior, and Samantha, who, being two years older than her brother, was nearly a generation older than Meghan.

The year her parents divorced, a new sitcom, *Married . . . with Children*, became a cult hit. Thomas Markle, who also lit the *General Hospital* sets for thirty-five years, was a lighting director for eleven episodes during the first season of *Married . . . with Children*; and from 1988 through 1996, logged 198 episodes as the show's cinematographer.

Some of Meghan's early years were spent at a house on the beach in Santa Monica, where, when Thomas threw parties, he would proudly show off his daughter to his show business friends. As times became even better, they moved back inland to the affluent Woodland Hills area in the Valley.

Thomas and Doria kept things amicable. Meghan was a frequent visitor to the *Married . . . with Children* set, where the stars would make a fuss over her. She was bitten by the acting bug before she became old enough to be inoculated against the hardships of a career in show business.

Thomas Markle had worked his way up to the top of his profession from his extremely humble beginnings in that small town in Pennsylvania. His childhood Christmas stockings had been filled with oranges; dinners were potatoes and Spam. "He invested in my future so I could have so much," Meghan recalls. And that future included a private school education, all expenses paid.

Meghan was enrolled at Hollywood's Little Red School House, a private grammar school for prekindergarten through sixth grade, known for its progressive educational bent. The school's stated mission is "to nurture the whole child within a diverse community, combining challenging academics with creative learning, where each child is known, encouraged, and valued."

Although the building has a distinctive red wooden facade and a farmer-in-the-dell type of steeple, the school's tuition is anything but homespun. Meghan attended the academy during the 1980s, when rates were lower, but the current costs range from about $18,800 for prekindergarten up to $22,700 for sixth grade, the final year.

Meghan's grammar school class picture hung on the white wall of her bedroom. Stars, hearts, and rainbows abounded on the matching Care Bears curtains and comforter that covered her single bed. Back then Meghan wore her dark hair in a fluffy ponytail or in two braids secured at the top and bottom of each plait.

Also hanging on her wall was the inspirational World War II *We Can Do It!* poster of Rosie the Riveter, with her hair neatly tucked under a polka-dotted red kerchief and the sleeves of her denim work shirt rolled up, one muscle-bound bare arm flexed to prove she's ready to get to work on the home front while the boys are off at war.

Social awareness came early. Meghan was raised to give back, as are so many who originally come from so little. At Thanksgiving, the family bought turkeys for homeless shelters and delivered meals to patients living in hospice care. At the age of thirteen, Meghan began volunteering in a soup kitchen on Los Angeles's Skid Row. Way out of her comfort zone, she "felt really scared" on her first day, recollecting years later, "I was young and it was rough and raw down there, and though I was with a great volunteer group, I just felt overwhelmed."

Meghan noticed the "quiet acts of grace" her parents would perform for those who had less, whether it was donating their spare change or even a personal acknowledgment of their shared humanity—a hug, a smile, or a pat on the back. It was a life lesson that stuck forever. Recalling how she was able to get past her fear during that first visit to Skid Row, Meghan said, "Never put yourself in a compromising situation, but once that is checked off the list, I think it's really important for us to remember that someone needs us, and that your act of giving [or] helping [or] doing can truly become an act of grace once you get out of your head."

Because it's what Meghan grew up with, she was raised with a social consciousness to do what she could about a situation, or at the very least to speak up when she knew something was wrong.

Meghan had been only ten years old when riots erupted in South Central L.A. in response to the violent police beating of a black motorist, Rodney King. A year later, when the four officers who so viciously beat King were acquitted, a second round of riots, along with arson and looting—known as the Rodney King Riots—lasted for six days, spreading throughout the Los Angeles metropolitan area. To ensure the children's safety during the riots, Meghan's school sent the students home. There was ash everywhere, settling on suburban lawns from the urban street fires.

"Oh my god, Mommy, it's snowing!" exclaimed the naive Meghan.

"No, Flower, it's not snow," her mother told her. "Get in the house."

Meghan's activism started in 1993, when she was a twelve-year-old elementary school student, as she was watching television commercials for a social studies assignment about messaging. First up, a spot for Robitussin cough syrup that referenced "Doctor Mom," which upset young Meghan because "it's always 'Mom does this and Mom does that.'"

Then the ad for Ivory dishwashing liquid came on the air. Meghan immediately took offense at the opening line of the voice-over: *Women are fighting greasy pots and pans.*

"I said, 'How could somebody say that?'"

After viewing the entire lineup, Meghan concluded that "just about one out of every three commercials is going to hurt somebody's feelings."

As for the Ivory spot, Meghan felt the premise was sexist, and she was spurred to do something about it after two of the boys in her class started yelling at the TV screen, "Yeah, that's where women belong—in the kitchen!"

Well!

Meghan spoke about the commercial at the United Nations on International Women's Day in 2015. She said, "I remember feeling shocked and angry and also just feeling so hurt; it just wasn't right, and something needed to be done. So I went home and told my dad what had happened, and he encouraged me to write letters. So I did: to the most powerful people I could think of."

Meghan's letter to the soap's manufacturer, Procter & Gamble, read: *So I was wondering if you would be able to change the commercial to "people."* She sent copies of it to civil rights lawyer Gloria Allred, then–first lady Hillary Clinton, and the cable TV channel Nickelodeon news anchor Linda Ellerbee. Ellerbee was so impressed that she sent a camera crew to meet Meghan.

Meghan told the Nickelodeon crew, "I don't think it is right for kids to grow up thinking that Mom does everything." She also encouraged others to speak up as she had done. "If you see something that you don't like, or are offended by, on television or any other place, write letters, and send them to the right people, and you can really make a difference, not just for yourself but for lots of other people."

A month or so later, Meghan saw the commercial again. The voice-over on the opening now said: *People are fighting greasy pots and pans.*

And years later as she recounted those events, Meghan told her UN audience, "It was at that moment that I realized the magnitude of my actions. At the age of eleven [*sic*], I had created my small level of impact by standing up for equality."

Ellerbee, who provided the *Nick News* footage to the television program *Inside Edition*, wasn't surprised that Meghan continues to be a voice for women all over the world. "It was absolutely clear that this young woman was strong in her beliefs," she told *Inside Edition*. "It didn't matter that she was eleven [*sic*] years old." [On-camera in the original Nickelodeon footage Meghan tells the interviewer that she's twelve.] "She believed in women and she believed in her own power and wasn't afraid to reach out and say, 'I want my power. I want my rights.'"

Every day after school, for ten years, Meghan would visit her father on the set of whichever show he was working on. Ironically, it was most often the sitcom with some of the most sexist jokes on prime time.

*Married . . . with Children* "was a really funny and perverse place for a little girl in a Catholic school uniform to grow up." Soft-core porn stars often did guest spots. "Just picture me with my curly hair and a gap in my teeth and my little school uniform with Keds on, looking up, like, 'Hi' at these very provocative women." The dialogue was racy and replete with double entendres. According to Meghan, "There were a lot of times my dad would say, 'Meg, why don't you go and help with the craft services room over there? This is just a little off-color for your eleven-year-old eyes.'" Craft services is the entity in the film industry that sets up the food for the cast and crew. All of Meghan's passions and skills—acting, being a foodie, learning how to find her key light (the main source of light on a film set)—were inculcated in that incubator of a sound stage, setting her on a yellow brick road toward her future.

"There I was, behind the scenes of a glossy soap opera and a TV sitcom, surrounded by famous actors and their glam teams, multimillion-dollar budgets, and crew lunches that always included filet mignon and enough sweets to make you think you were at Willy Wonka's Chocolate Factory," Meghan later wrote. Of course anyone who's been around actors, especially those who work in film, where it's a truism that the camera makes one appear ten pounds heavier, knows that actors aren't the ones eating all that steak and candy. As Meghan correctly noted, it's the *crew* eating all that heavenly stuff.

But the opportunity to hang around so many actors—whether or not they noshed—and to watch the process of filming from the ground up whetted Meghan's appetite for the profession. Aware of how much work it took, how long the hours were, and how grueling the pace—despite the "glam squads" with their tote bags crammed full of hair products and their little aprons stuffed with makeup brushes of every size and shape—she would be able to choose a career as an actor with her eyes wide open.

# Goodbye, Mummy

It was a late Saturday afternoon in November 1996, and the sky outside Kensington Palace was already growing dark. As usual, Harry was home for the weekend from Ludgrove. The twelve-year-old prince was napping fitfully with his head in his mother's lap as she chatted with Simone Simmons, a close friend the princess liked to refer to as "a special lady." The women had already enjoyed two pots of comforting herbal tea, but Simone had no words of comfort for Diana.

Simone was a psychic "energy healer" who often came to KP to smudge the rooms, cleansing them of troublesome spirits, conflict, anger, or illness. By 1996, she and Diana were conversing daily; and Simone had even taught the princess some of her healing techniques, which Diana practiced on Harry and William when they were under the weather. Both young princes were intrigued by the astrologers and spiritualists consulted by their mother.

"I don't know, Diana," Simone replied. "I see four people in a car and a terrible crash. I don't know who they are."

The previous summer, Diana had fallen madly in love with Hasnat Khan, an accomplished heart surgeon she met while visiting a friend at Royal Brompton Hospital. But coming from a traditional Muslim background, Khan was never entirely comfortable being the clandestine lover of the most famous woman in the world. Nevertheless, convinced that he was the love of her life, one night Diana asked Khan to marry her and move into Kensington Palace so he could become better acquainted with Harry and William. But Dr. Khan didn't want to be a family man—at least being a father to Diana's sons was not on his agenda. According to royal biographer Christopher Andersen, he found the idea of a secret marriage ridiculous. Khan's family would only accept a Pakistani Muslim bride for him, even though Diana had traveled to his homeland several times to meet the surgeon's relatives and immerse herself in his culture. She was studying the Koran and her closet was filled with *shalwar kameez*, Pakistan's traditional ensemble worn both by women and men, consisting of a long tunic and loose, flowing pants.

Andersen's biography *William and Kate* chronicles the end of the princess's romance with Hasnat Khan. Evidently, Diana had gone so far as to have her butler Paul Burrell secretly make inquiries to determine whether a Catholic priest would marry her to Dr. Khan. After reiterating her desire for Khan to move into Kensington Palace so her sons could "know you the way I know you," a "flabbergasted" Khan replied that the only way he could see them "having a normal life together" was if Diana moved to Pakistan. But that was an absolute deal breaker. "I cannot be away from my boys," Diana insisted. "They need me now more than ever." That night, Khan ended their on-again, off-again relationship.

In the summer of 1997, the Egyptian-born Mohamed Al Fayed, who owned Harrods department store, was enthusiastically playing matchmaker between Diana and his divorced playboy son Dodi, an erstwhile filmmaker.

During a six-week whirlwind romance—much of it spent at Mohamed's villa on the French Riviera or aboard his luxury yacht, the *Jonikal*, the forty-two-year-old Dodi hotly wooed Diana, showering her with lavish gifts, which she could have afforded to purchase on her own if she desired. What she basked in was his indulgent attention, abetted by his father's unsubtle pandering. Diana had recently redecorated her Kensington Palace digs; and Dodi's father, "Mo," had stocked the game room with toys and games from Harrods. No pressure there.

Dodi's much younger siblings, Omar, Jasmine, and Camilla, already got on well with Harry and William. While Dodi romanced Harry's mum, the twelve-year-old video game addict hung out with the youngest Al Fayeds and proved himself the undisputable king of Sonic the Hedgehog.

Maybe . . . just maybe . . . an interdenominational Brady Bunch could be formed from the families of the princess and the playboy. What a coup it would be for the Egyptian Muslim Mohamed if his son were to wed the former Princess of Wales! As it was, she had already created something of a PR nightmare for Buckingham Palace by dating back-to-back Muslim men.

The long-lensed paparazzi couldn't get enough photos of Di and Dodi. Because the princess had recovered from her eating disorder and from one angle a bikini picture appeared to show a slightly rounded belly, Fleet Street went nuts. *Was Diana pregnant?*

Did any of them pay attention during biology class? Even if the lovers had sex on the first date, Diana had not even known Dodi long enough to show a pregnancy in July 1997. Speculation increased further: Were Diana and Dodi engaged?

It was nearly impossible for them to enjoy a holiday, though, thanks to the intrusive paparazzi. After Diana was stripped of her HRH title, she also lost the right to a security detail from Scotland Yard. She wished to disengage herself from the permanent spotlight; it was rumored she might relocate to America. But she could never leave the country with her sons, both royal princes and one the heir to the throne. And Diana had no intention of moving anywhere without them. According to essayist Clive James, "Diana believed, against all the evidence, that there was some enchanted place called Abroad, where she could be understood and where she could lead a more normal life."

Harry and William spent the second half of their 1997 summer holiday with their father and the Queen at Balmoral. Because they were photographed everywhere they went with their mother, Her Majesty believed it was vital for the princes to enjoy some privacy in the remote Highland enclave.

On the morning of Saturday, August 30, Diana phoned Scotland from Paris, where she and Dodi were staying at the Hôtel Ritz, another property owned by Mohamed Al Fayed. Diana had intended to reunite with her boys that day, but Dodi had made the snap decision to spend the night in the City of Lights instead.

William was the one who got on the phone with his mum to tell her all about the brothers' wonderful holiday at Balmoral. They couldn't wait to see her again, he told her. *Again* was supposed to be *tomorrow*.

Harry didn't get to speak to his mother. Which means he was never able to say goodbye.

And *tomorrow* never came.

Simone Simmons had a vision in November 1996 of a "terrible crash" in Paris. Another of Diana's friends, the clairvoyant Rita Rogers, had warned Dodi not to go to Paris on August 30, 1997, because she had a vision of him in danger in a tunnel there.

Late that evening, Diana's usual driver was dispatched from the Ritz in her Range Rover as a decoy to lure the waiting paparazzi away. A little while later, Dodi's driver was sent on a second decoy run.

Henri Paul was the Ritz's deputy chief of security. That night he was off duty and had spent several hours drinking pastis. He had also been taking the antidepressants Prozac and Tiapradal. With no other driver available, at the last minute he was pressed into service to get behind the wheel of the $170,000 armored Mercedes 220SL that the Ritz employed to ferry anxious VIP guests. Henri Paul did not possess a traditional chauffeur's license. He was credentialed to drive that armored Mercedes, but did not have the special license required under French law to drive *high-powered* vehicles.

Late that Saturday night, with a blood alcohol level that was three times above the legal limit for drinking and driving, combined with the meds he'd ingested, Henri Paul was speeding through Paris's Pont de l'Alma tunnel, pursued by a phalanx of paparazzi, when he lost control of the Mercedes and struck a pillar. The costly armored car was crushed like a can of soda. Henri Paul and Dodi were killed instantly. According to prosecutors, the speedometer on the mangled dashboard was frozen at 121 miles per hour.

Diana was treated at the crash site but lost consciousness soon afterward. She was rushed the four miles to the Pitié-Salpêtrière Hospital in critical condition with severe internal injuries; every attempt was made to save her.

The only survivor was Diana's bodyguard Trevor Rees-Jones. He was also the only one who had been wearing a seat belt.

It was shortly after three A.M. on Sunday, August 31, when the British embassy informed the royal family that Diana was gone.

Charles reportedly wailed like a character from a Greek tragedy.

The Queen decided to let the young princes slumber on. In her view, there would be so much to deal with when they awoke that a few more hours of blissful unawareness couldn't hurt.

William awakened to find his papa seated at the foot of his bed, his eyes red and swollen from crying. Together they agreed to deliver the devastating news to Harry.

Of all times to maintain that stiff upper lip, when two young boys were reeling with shock over the sudden and tragic death of their mother, the senior members of the royal family made the determination that the best thing for the princes would be to carry on as if nothing major had happened. So they went to church at

Craithie Kirk as if it were any other Sunday morning at Balmoral, in the belief the boys would derive comfort from their faith. But now that the news of Diana's demise had been released, all eyes were on them, expecting a reaction. Harry and William had been encouraged to cry in private; they knew their duty as royals meant expressing no public emotion. What an impossible request in such a situation! When no mention whatever was made in church of Diana's passing, Harry asked, "Are you sure Mummy is dead?" The young prince was in shock: numb and silent, refusing to leave the side of his nanny, Tiggy.

Charles had the television in the nursery removed so the boys wouldn't have to see the endless loops of devastating news footage.

As Harry and William fished the River Dee in mournful silence, down in London, people gathered by the thousands to pay their respects, leaving an ocean of floral tributes at the gates of Kensington Palace. They were shocked by Diana's sudden death and perceived the Queen's refusal to curtail her Scottish holiday as a passive-aggressive gesture from a hostile former mother-in-law. The Queen, they believed, was ignoring a nation in pain.

Her Majesty's perspective was different, however. She believed she was protecting her precious grandsons by prolonging their privacy. For the first time in her life she was placing the feelings of her family above duty.

But Fleet Street agreed with the public. Tabloid headlines eviscerated the monarch. WHERE IS THE QUEEN WHEN HER COUNTRY NEEDS HER? the *Daily Mail* demanded to know. SPEAK TO US, MA'AM—YOUR PEOPLE ARE SUFFERING, declared *The Mirror*.

Unaware that the Windsors were weeping their eyes out behind the heavy doors of Balmoral, the *Daily Mirror*, noting that the royals had absented themselves from their subjects, asked WHY CAN'T THE ROYAL FAMILY SHOW ITS GRIEF? Even the pro-royal *Daily Express* urged the monarchy to SHOW US YOU CARE.

Opinion polls taken at the time revealed that 70 percent of

Britons believed that the Queen's refusal to return to Buckingham Palace damaged the reputation of the monarchy as an institution, with 25 percent stating that it was time to bring the monarchy itself to an end. If the sovereign couldn't be there to comfort her subjects in a time of national crisis, what good was she?

But now Britain was seemingly on the verge of a revolt because the flag at Buckingham Palace had not been lowered to half-mast. The official explanation was that because Diana was no longer a titled member of the royal family at the time of her death, protocol didn't require this gesture of recognition. But that rationale seemed churlish and tone-deaf, like something out of a classic fairy tale—as if the elderly queen remained envious, even in death, of Diana's youth and popularity.

Nearly a week after Diana's demise, Queen Elizabeth II caved to public pressure and the urging of her prime minister, Tony Blair. Although she believed bereavement was a private matter, on September 5, 1997, she returned to Buckingham Palace, where she delivered a televised address to a nation united in grief, speaking as their queen and as a grandmother.

At Kensington Palace, Harry joined William and their father on a walkabout in front of the black and gold iron gates. Kneeling to view some of the cards that accompanied the sea of condolence bouquets, they were profoundly touched, not only by the outpouring of tributes but by the thousands of people who waited to see them. The boys behaved royally, holding back their tears. To the sound of gentle applause, the three Windsor princes shook hands with the crowd, and a woman shouted, "We love you!" as a mourner handed Harry and William individual calla lilies.

The most challenging assignment of all for the young princes was participating in their mother's funeral cortege on September sixth. William, then fifteen, was adamant in his refusal to walk, certain he would not be able to keep his emotions in check. It was Prince Philip who persuaded him, explaining that while he might not feel up to it in the days that immediately followed his mother's death, it would be his only opportunity to escort Diana on her final journey, and later in his life he might look back and regret the decision not to do so. Besides, Philip urged, if William walked behind his mother's caisson, then Harry could be persuaded to walk alongside him; if he didn't walk, Harry would never have the courage to make that lonely pilgrimage on his own. He knew whereof he spoke. At age sixteen, Philip had walked in the very public funeral procession of his beloved older sister, Princess Cecilie of Greece and Denmark, after her tragic death in a plane crash. He managed to change the young princes' minds.

Diana's casket was draped in the yellow, red, and blue royal standard, the Queen's official flag. The caisson bearing it was drawn by three teams of coal black horses from the King's Troop Royal Artillery. As the carriage halted before Kensington Palace, the television cameras panned to show to the worldwide audience of 2.5 billion viewers—the largest audience for any televised event ever—the deluge of love for Diana from all over the world. The palace and the surrounding buildings and monuments seemed to float amid a sea of bouquets of every color and size.

The sight was enough to crack the hardest heart. But undoubtedly the most poignant of all was the display atop the casket itself: an arrangement of white roses and Casablanca lilies bearing a white card on which Prince Harry had written a single word. *Mummy.*

Harry walked between his father and his uncle Charles, Diana's brother. As they reached the protective shadow of Horse Guards Arch, shielded from public view, the earl gave Harry a reassuring pat on the shoulder.

No cameras were permitted to focus their lenses on Harry and William once the princes were inside Westminster Abbey. Harry broke down as their mother's casket passed. William hugged him protectively.

Diana had raised them to be normal boys after all.

# [*You Gotta Have*] *Heart*

A stone's throw from the American Film Institute, which is known for preserving the country's illustrious cinematic history, for educating filmmakers, and for its lists of the top 100 films, sits the 112-year-old Immaculate Heart High School. Founded by Catholic nuns, this all-girls college prep school "dedicated to the intellectual, spiritual, moral, and social development of young women" sprawls over an enviably beautiful campus. Shaded by palm trees, amid acres of lush greenery, fewer than seven hundred students, aged eleven to eighteen, attend middle school and high school in Spanish Colonial–style stucco buildings with red-tiled roofs. The sparkling swimming pool would even tempt someone who hates gym class.

Tuition for the 2016–17 school year was $15,700, placing it in the mid-priced range of private schools in that area of Hollywood and Beverly Hills; however, according to Immaculate Heart's president Maureen Diekmann, they "have some very wealthy students, and some who are financially challenged." To that end, Immaculate Heart provides a million dollars a year in grants so that less-wealthy girls from the Los Angeles area are able to be educated there.

The school aims to create "a mixture of the traditional and the innovative," providing the students with a balance "of discipline and freedom; of play and work; of concern for things of the heart as well as of the mind; and of a readiness to create and to celebrate."

Because Immaculate Heart is a parochial school, part of its mission is "to share in the teaching ministry of the Catholic Church by creating a learning environment where students can, with Mary as their model, mature in their faith as they reflect on their special roles as members of the Christian community."

Not all students who attend Immaculate Heart are Catholic, and the staff makes a point of stating that they respect the religious and ethnic diversity of the student body.

Meghan Markle is not Catholic, nor was she raised in the Catholic faith.

It seems clear, however, that Immaculate Heart's philosophy helped shape the woman she grew up to be. "The school assists parents by helping their daughters to develop in such a way that they will become women of great heart and of right conscience; knowledgeable and concerned about the earth and the global community in which they live; creative as problem-solvers; capable of building on their appreciation of and acquired skills in the humanities and sciences; aware that learning is a lifetime endeavor; and convinced that, ultimately, all must develop within themselves a capacity for integrity, wisdom, humor, joy, peace and love, so as to 'make gentle the life of this world.'"

Among the other alumna of this school, which has a cuddly panda as its mascot, are the supermodel Tyra Banks and the legendary television actress Mary Tyler Moore, who "turned the world on with her smile" during her eponymous long-running series.

When Meghan entered the middle school at Immaculate Heart, she would have pledged "as a young woman of integrity" to abide by the school's honor code, which included the promise to respect the property of the school and of other students; not to cheat; never to steal from her classmates, nor to plagiarize the ideas of others and present them as her own; and to always assume responsibility for her own actions.

She took the school's philosophy to heart. One alumna recalled with tears in her eyes an incident that occurred when she was in seventh grade at Immaculate Heart. Meghan, who was a year above her and didn't know her, confronted a bunch of mean girls from the senior class who were bullying the underclassman. "We don't do that here," she said.

During her three years of middle school, Meghan received a well-rounded education. Fine and performing arts classes included an appreciation of culturally diverse forms of expression and an awareness of the importance of the arts in all areas of the school's curriculum. Being health conscious didn't just mean exercising and learning to eat well, although one can see where some of the seeds of Meghan's "foodie" persona were planted. It meant learning to become ethically and socially responsible, as well as being an accountable steward of the planet.

At that age, Meghan was also learning financial responsibility. Despite enjoying the privileges of a posh private school education, she was thirteen when she started her first job. Paula Sheftel was Meghan's former boss at Humphrey Yogart in the leafy Los Angeles suburb of Sherman Oaks, where Meghan earned minimum wage serving frozen yogurt. Even then, as Ms. Sheftel recollected, Meghan's outgoing personality served her well. The bubbly young teen succeeded because of her ability to relate to the customers and to work well with the rest of the staff.

Even as she scooped yogurt, Meghan was already practicing the other key focuses of Immaculate Heart's Middle School curriculum, among them thinking critically, being an effective communicator—which meant listening to others as well as speaking thoughtfully and eloquently—and being a constructive member of society.

But one seventh-grade assignment completely tripped her up.

In her English class, Meghan had to complete a mandatory census. It required her to check only one box describing her ethnicity. She sat paralyzed, pen poised above the form. Curly haired, freckled, pale complexioned. Biracial. To check the box for either black or white was to reject one of her parents—to choose one over the other. One half of *herself* over the other.

Her teacher, noticing that she had stopped completing the form, came over to her desk. Meghan admitted her consternation. The teacher told her to check the box for Caucasian—"because that's how you look, Meghan."

Meghan couldn't do it. She put down her pen. Not, she said, as an act of defiance, but as a symptom of her confusion.

"I couldn't bring myself to do that, to picture the pit-in-her-belly sadness my mother would feel if she were to find out. So I didn't tick a box. I left my identity blank—a question mark, an absolute incomplete—much like I felt."

When Meghan got home she told her father what had happened at school that day. She had never before seen him angry; but that night she watched "the blotchiness of his skin crawling from pink to red. It made the green of his eyes pop and his brow was weighted at the thought of his daughter being prey to ignorance. Growing up in a homogenous community in Pennsylvania, the concept of marrying an African American woman was not [in] the cards for my dad. But he saw beyond what was put in front of him in that small-sized (and perhaps, small-minded) town, and he wanted me to see beyond that census placed in front of me. He wanted me to find my own truth."

Thomas Markle then told his daughter something that has stayed with her for the rest of her life. He said, "If that happens again, you draw your own box."

Two hundred and forty-five credits are required to graduate from Immaculate Heart's high school, plus four years of community service. Among the requisite theology courses is a semester in "Contemporary Moral Issues." Students can also avail themselves of Advanced Placement courses in the traditional liberal arts classes, as well as computer science. "Pandas Explore" is an extracurricular educational travel program for the students, from the Close Up domestic excursions to New York and Washington, DC, to international destinations such as Rome and Belize.

Because Meghan graduated from a school that offers such a banquet of academics and extracurricular activities, it's all the more insulting that some members of the British press and racist Internet trolls later felt compelled to paint her, condescendingly, viciously, and incorrectly, as some sort of slum bunny.

Meghan was *always* passionate about social justice, according to Maria Pollia, one of her former theology teachers and a woman Meghan has also numbered among her mentors.

Pollia taught her young students that "life is about putting others' needs above your own fears," a lesson that Meghan took to heart that first day she entered the Skid Row soup kitchen and one that has remained with her ever since.

Ms. Pollia recollected that Meghan also "had this compassion for homeless people, for gang members, for people who were on the margins of society. She took our social justice teaching very seriously and wanted to not just study about it but to be a part of making the world a more open and welcoming place for those that the rest of society had ignored." Pollia taught the girls of Immaculate Heart that people in soup kitchens and shelters were hungry not just for food but for human contact and to be respected as a fellow human being. Just saying "good morning" to them was really important.

Christine Knudsen, who taught one of Meghan's senior electives classes, remembered Meghan's spunkiness and feistiness, along with her passion for singing and acting. But there was more to her even then—an inner depth "which kind of moved into all of her other subjects."

Meghan was fourteen years old when her best friend Suzy Arkadani was called to the principal's office. Suzy's father, a garage owner, had been shot by a deranged Vietnam veteran who had just murdered his own family. The man had burst into Mr. Arkadani's garage and sprayed the place with bullets, and now Arkadani was fighting for his life. Meghan, as close to Suzy as a family member, was the first of Suzy's classmates to comfort her and was the only one who accompanied Suzy to the hospital. Meghan sat with the family by Suzy's father's bedside, praying he would pull through. Matt Arkadani's injuries left him paralyzed; but Suzy's mother, Sonia, credits his survival at least in part to Meghan's prayers and devotion to the family in their hour of need.

Years earlier, Sonia had taped Lady Diana Spencer's wedding to Prince Charles on her VCR. She showed it to Suzy and Meghan, who later became as impressed by Diana's humanitarian work as by her glamour. According to Sonia Arkadani, the teens would see stories about Diana on television and choose to follow her example in their own way, by volunteering in a soup kitchen or collecting clothes and toys for children who were less fortunate than they were.

MEGHAN'S LIFELONG INTEREST in philanthropy was also sparked by the trips she took with her mother to remote and impoverished parts of the globe. It was important to Doria, who worked as a travel agent for a time to make ends meet, that Meghan gain the experience and understanding of how others lived.

In Oaxaca, Mexico, Meghan watched children not much younger than she was, playing in the dirt roads and peddling Chiclets for a few extra pesos to help feed their families. She was only ten when her mother took her to Jamaica. But they didn't go to the five-star Jamaica Inn in Ocho Rios, where Meghan would eventually wed her first husband. Instead, Doria took her to see the slums. For a little girl from California's San Fernando Valley, it was an awakening. Meghan's brown eyes welled with tears and fear.

"Don't be scared, Flower," Doria told her daughter. "Be aware, but don't be afraid."

In a prescient snapshot taken in 1996 when Meghan visited London with Ninaki Priddy, her best friend at the time, the California girls posed in their summer clothes and sunglasses in front of Buckingham Palace. Most American tourists in London have a similar photo.

But only *one* would grow up to marry the grandson of the Queen of England.

As a high schooler, Meghan could resemble the proverbial girl next door in a cardigan with flat-ironed hair or could be completely free spirited and bohemian. In a striking photo taken on one of the campus lawns with five of her classmates, Meghan poses with untamed curls, exhibiting the same wide smile and zest for life that she still has twenty years later. Five of the students are wearing the full Immaculate Heart uniform of cardigans or sleeveless vests, white blouses, and pleated skirts, with white socks and sneakers. Meghan is the only one who dared to be different; she isn't wearing a sweater over her blouse. In fact, she seems to have given her shirt a blouson effect, so that of all six girls in the snapshot, she alone has made the effort to transform a Catholic school uniform into a fashion statement.

A friend who knew Meghan at Immaculate Heart recollected that she "was bubbly, optimistic, and positive. She was also very focused and had her eye on the prize—she knew where she wanted to go to college and she knew she wanted to do drama." Meghan was even a TA in her high school drama classes. "Most kids our age wouldn't have felt as confident in their skills." Her old friend added, "She had the talent and focus to back it up; and you could tell she knew the work it would take and she was willing to [do it]. She was a role model and was inspiring. She had an ability to be effortlessly kind."

Catherine Knight, another Immaculate Heart classmate who had known Meghan since middle school, chose three words to describe her old friend: "kind, generous, enthusiastic," all borne out in the lengthy bubbly compliment Meghan gave Ms. Knight when she signed her yearbook one year.

"Harry is lucky to have her," enthused yet another old friend from Meghan's high school days. "No one who knows Meghan could have a bad word to say about her. She is the kindest person, and incredibly smart. She doesn't buy into Hollywood fakeness. She's a genuinely good person who cares about others."

As Meghan had wanted to be an actress from an early age, she took several drama classes and performed the leading role in many of the school plays produced in Immaculate Heart's gymnasium, including the role of Daddy Warbucks's secretary Grace in the musical *Annie* and that of an aspiring actress in *Stage Door*. Former classmates recall that Meghan's rendition of the song "Nothing" from *A Chorus Line*, about transcending the damage done by a negative high school drama teacher, was unquestionably of a professional caliber. Meghan also scored the lead in *Damn Yankees* at Loyola High School of Los Angeles, a neighboring all-boys school. She was what is known in theater parlance as a triple threat—an actress-singer-dancer. Meghan even had tap-dancing chops, which she put to use in Immaculate Heart's 1998 production of the British musical *Stepping Out*, about a group of working-class Englishwomen (and one man) whose lives become improved in every way by attending a weekly tap class in a dingy church social hall.

Maria Pollia remembered that Meghan was highly determined

to become a success. It was "not a frivolous pursuit, not 'oh, I'm going to be a movie star.'"

An academy that attracts the children of well-heeled, if not celebrity parents, also attracted instructors with Hollywood credits of their own. Immaculate Heart's drama teacher Gigi Perreau's three-decade film career began at the age of two when she played Greer Garson's daughter in *Madame Curie*. Speaking to *The Telegraph*, a British daily, Ms. Perreau had nothing but praise for her former student. "A lovely girl even then; and very hardworking. She was very dedicated. I knew she would be something special."

Ms. Perreau not only taught Meghan, she directed her. Unlike some students, who get bored with the necessarily repetitive weeks or months of rehearsal, or whose stage fright gets the better of them in performance, if Meghan had any opening-night jitters, she managed to transcend them. According to Ms. Perreau, "We never had a moment's problem with her; she was spot-on, learnt her lines when she had to," and was "very dedicated, very focused." Of Meghan's performance in *Annie*, Ms. Perreau recalled, "She was particularly delightful . . . I remember her being very excited and nervous about her song."

Years later, when Meghan and Prince Harry spoke to the BBC after they announced their engagement, Meghan explained to the interviewer Mishal Husain that becoming a member of the royal family would give her an even bigger "voice" when it came to her humanitarian work. So how might that pan out; what could be a bigger voice than acting? Harry joked, "Sing!"

Meghan burst out laughing and demurred, responding, "Can you imagine? No, I'm *not* a singer." But to win those leads in her high school musical productions when Meghan was in her teens, she must have had a creditable soprano with a strong "belt" voice, as it's known in the theater.

Certainly the experience of watching the rehearsals and performances of soap and sitcom actors every day after school provided both a foundation and a grounding, not only for Meghan's technique, but for her work ethic.

Meghan's father, already an award-winning television lighting designer by then, would volunteer to light Immaculate Heart's school plays, somewhat akin to a dad who's a Major League slugger helping coach the softball team.

Inevitably, there were a few snide comments that Meghan won her roles (whatever Meghan wanted, Meghan got, to paraphrase Lola in *Damn Yankees*) because of her father's A-list volunteerism.

One of the detractors was her own half sister Samantha, seventeen years Meghan's senior. Samantha, an attractive blue-eyed blonde who had lived for a time with her mother in rural New Mexico after Roslyn and Thomas Markle went their separate ways, also had ambitions to become a professional actress. But proximity is an element in the equation; and there's a vast difference between growing up in New Mexico and in the heart of Hollywood.

However, it wasn't always a certainty that Meghan *would* eventually become a professional actress. She was also inspired by Immaculate Heart's humanitarian focus. "I think I was able to share a lot of my theories about giving back when you've been very fortunate in the industry as I was," said Ms. Perreau. "Hopefully many of my students got that compassion and desire to do something worthwhile with their lives. I wasn't sure which direction Meghan would ultimately be going on because she also had interests in humanitarian activities, and she seemed to be extremely well rounded and focused on her future."

*Ambition* is not a dirty word. Every day Meghan saw firsthand how it paid off for the sitcom and soap opera actors and those who worked in the technical aspects of the film and television industry. She recognized what was required to succeed, in both time and tenacity. And she was more than willing to put in the work.

In Meghan's senior yearbook, the words that her classmates

used to describe her were "classy girl." The phrase was printed on the frame that rimmed her California license plate as well.

She agonized over what to choose as a yearbook quote, as if it were her epitaph. It became a dead heat between "Shoot for the moon. Even if you don't hit it, you'll land among the stars," and a chestnut often attributed to Eleanor Roosevelt: "Women are like tea bags. They don't realize how strong they are until they're in hot water." Meghan ended up selecting the first option. In retrospect, she trusted her gut all along.

In 1998, the Homecoming Week theme in November paid homage to fashions of the past. Students strutting the halls in Fonzie-style leather motorcycle jackets from the sitcom *Happy Days* mingled with classmates channeling the 1960s in bell-bottoms and hippie fringe, seventies disco duds, and the wide shoulders and leggings of those who were nostalgic for their fairly recent childhood of the 1980s and just wanted their MTV.

During halftime at the Homecoming football game on Friday night, seventeen-year-old Meghan was crowned Homecoming Queen, proving even then that she could wear a tiara with poise and grace. She was chosen in a two-step process: boys from local private schools nominated girls from other private schools, who were then interviewed by a committee that made the final selection. When all of the girls in the court were brought out to the fifty-yard line during halftime, the name of the Homecoming Queen was announced from among them.

Meghan walked a red carpet flanked by her court and a phalanx of knights from their brother school St. Francis High, with swords in hand. After the ceremony, the entire court processed off the field in classic convertibles.

How classically Southern California.

That evening, Meghan posed for her Homecoming Dance photo in a pale blue satin strapless gown, cradling a long-stemmed bouquet. Beside her stood her prom date Danny Segura, a handsome dark-haired St. Francis High student. Speaking in 2017 about the teenage Meghan, Danny called her "awesome," and he would use the same word to describe the Meghan of today.

Meghan encouraged Danny to audition for his first high school musical when he was fifteen. "I was hooked from that point," he reminisced. Although he was her date for the Homecoming Dance, they were just friends. Danny still works in theater, and he and Meghan still remain friends. She also dated his older brother Luis when she was in high school. Luis, who was never bitten by the theater bug, eventually married, had two kids, and went into real estate.

Even then Meghan was keenly aware of the minutest details of style, so the V-shape of her sparkling necklace was a mirror image of her glittering tiara. She never could have dreamt that it would be another twenty years before she would *officially* be permitted to don a tiara by marrying into the House of Windsor! According to royal protocol, only *married* women are permitted to wear one.

The theme of Saturday night's Homecoming Dance was "The Glory of the Knight," paying tribute to the St. Francis team, who had been victorious under the Friday-night lights in the football game against the Chaminade Eagles from a rival school. The St. Francis Knights boogied the night away with the pandas of Immaculate Heart to the techno beats of the 1980s, with a few slow dances thrown in to kindle some chastely romantic swaying.

The lessons Immaculate Heart inculcated in Meghan paid off so well that she has become an inspiration to the students who came after her, the girls who now roam the white-painted hallways ringed with shoulder-height blue lockers.

They refer to Meghan as "one of our sisters." A curly-haired blonde said she was proud of her because "she knows what she's saying; and she's definitely not afraid to say what she needs to say, and to stand up for whatever's right." Another blonde agreed that "we're following in her footsteps."

According to Callie Webb, the school's director of communications, they "were so proud of her speech in 2015 to the UN, as a UN Women ambassador, about gender equality," which the students watched in their ethics class.

Public speaking may come naturally to Meghan, but it's also part of the Immaculate Heart curriculum. The current students are proud to claim a poised and well-spoken future princess as an alumna and are as excited about Meghan's activism as they are about her future as a member of the royal family, having avidly followed every detail of her romance with Prince Harry since the news broke. No matter how early these Los Angelenos have to wake up to watch the royal wedding of one of their own, they'll be glued to the television with a cup of tea.

It's something else Meghan and Harry have in common: a single-sex secondary school education at an elite preparatory academy that focuses on instilling honor, integrity, and morality in impressionable young minds and hearts.

# The Playing Fields of Eton

## Acting Out

Charles knew that Harry needed a breather. Managing their public and private grief for Diana was a daunting process. William and Harry had moved into York House with their father; and he was struggling at being both papa and mummy to them. It had been up to Tiggy to help the boys navigate the world in the wake of their mother's death. She accompanied them as they followed the legendary Beaufort hunt on foot and wandered the empty rooms of Kensington Palace, selecting which of Diana's personal effects they wished to retain as mementos. Harry initially chose his mum's engagement ring with its stunning eighteen-carat sapphire surrounded by diamonds; and William selected her Cartier Tank watch; but the princes agreed that whichever of them got engaged first would give the ring to his fiancée, so a swap might happen in the future.

In November 1997, two months after Diana was laid to rest at Althorp, Charles treated Harry to a much-needed break, taking him along on a state visit to South Africa. One of the highlights for the starstruck thirteen-year-old, who was becoming as interested in beautiful girls as he was in all things military, was the opportunity to meet the Spice Girls at a concert in Pretoria for Nelson Mandela. Posing for the obligatory photo op between Emma Bunton (Baby Spice) and Victoria Beckham (Posh Spice), Harry declared it the best day of his life. Harry had also urged his papa to take him to see Rorke's Drift, site of a legendary battle between British forces and Zulu warriors. One of Harry's favorite movies was *Zulu*, and he had become fascinated by the real story behind it. It was at Rorke's Drift where Harry solemnly told his papa that one day he too planned to fight for Queen and country.

Harry had another life-changing experience during this trip, when Tiggy took him on safari in Botswana while Charles was busy on official duties. Harry was enthralled with Africa's expansive red earth, its magical wildlife, and the spectacular sunsets of purple, red, and gold.

Botswana, in particular, captured Harry's heart. Two years later when he was fifteen, he came back, with Tiggy acting as chaperone. It would be the first of several return visits.

FROM MRS. MYNORS' to Wetherby to Ludgrove, and now to the venerable Eton, Harry was following William from school to school as if he were tracking his elder brother's footsteps on the beach or stepping into the imprints he'd made in the snow. The Waleses had insisted their sons attend the lofty institution founded in 1440 by Henry VI. Not only has Eton educated several royal boys, but it's also produced nineteen prime ministers and even graduated a number of other renowned redheads, including Harry's uncle Charles Spencer and film stars Eddie Redmayne and Damian Lewis.

On September 2, 1998, just thirteen days shy of his fourteenth birthday, Harry became an F-tit, a first-year Etonian, at Manor House, the same residency house where William was a student. In fact William acted as his younger brother's tour guide, starting with the locales where Harry would spend the lion's share of his downtime, such as the common room and the games room. Harry noticed that the F-tits' locker room, where they were required to deposit their schoolbooks and outdoor boots, looked straight onto the street, offering a clear view to both tourists and paparazzi— quite unlike the sheltered atmosphere at Ludgrove. Newspapers were not verboten at Eton, so Harry could easily read what was being written about his family.

Nestled in the town of the same name, across the Thames from Windsor, Eton College (which is actually what Americans would call a private high school, and what the English would call a public school) has its own slang, rituals, and dress code. The boys still resemble charming post-Edwardians out of the pages of *Brideshead Revisited*, in pinstriped trousers, long black tailcoats with waistcoats, and white shirts with a stiff white collar and tie. The lingo conjures Harry Potter. Scholars who live on campus are known as Collagers, while the Oppidans live in boardinghouses in the town, which, with its half-timbered facades in the High Street, still bears some of the elements of a quaint English village. Instructors are *beaks*, and a centrally located lamppost on the campus is known as the *burning bush*. The *abracadabra* is the school's timetable, and the famed rowers are *wet bobs*.

After chapel on Sundays, Harry and his mates would walk across the bridge into town, where they might grab a Big Mac and catch the latest action flick at the cinema on Windsor High Street. If they felt really daring and were flush with dosh, they'd sneak off to the Windsor races. When they were upperclassmen, they would slink into a pub or meet up with the girls who attended St. Mary's School Ascot in Berkshire. St. Mary's motto was "Women in time will come to do much."

Harry and company couldn't get into too much trouble, however, because they had to be back in their respective houses at Eton by eight-fifteen on Sunday evening.

It didn't take long before Harry became comfortable enough at Eton to slip back into the role of class clown. He was a poorer student than William, but a much better athlete. Where Harry excelled, however, was as a prankster. He would spend an entire class hiding behind the drapes, revealing himself only when the beak was about to mark him absent, after calling his name from the roll several times, only to hear muffled giggles in reply. A less innocuous jest involved balancing a book on the top of a door so that it would bean the beak on the head when he opened it, convulsing Harry and his classmates with laughter. Harry never selected a volume that was heavy enough to wound someone, but it certainly startled the hell out of the victim.

The prince never got caught and no one ever ratted him out. Perhaps royalty has its privileges. And the more untouchable Harry became, the more he pushed his luck. Unfortunately, his grades were the consequences of his actions. By the end of Harry's E, or second, year at Eton, he was in the bottom group of students.

Harry was behaving more like a court jester than a prince, but his shenanigans were the only tools he seemed to have for coping with the unimaginably awful loss of his mother. He was unable to mourn her when he should have been able to and needed to, but had been forced to suppress his emotions instead; and now he was acting up and acting out. Like his mum, Harry craved attention and affection. But like her, he also had a self-destructive streak.

By 2001, Harry was in his third year of high school—and was unsupervised when he needed it most. William was taking his gap year between high school graduation and university; and their father was either off on official business or at Birkhall, the Queen Mother's cottage at the edge of Balmoral.

Charles had, however, given his consent to the transformation of his downstairs cellar at Highgrove into a clubhouse-cum-disco for Harry and his aristocratic Gloucestershire pals, the punning, rhyming Glosse Posse. Club H's two cavernous subterranean rooms with their vaulted ceilings and state-of-the-art audio system were a teenage boy's dream. Cream-colored sofas provided cushy seating. The walls of the disco room were painted black, which would have made the Rolling Stones proud. A portrait of the Abdicator, Harry's disgraced ancestor Edward VIII, was hung upside down in the loo.

Although Charles had leveled a strict no-smoking, no-alcohol policy in Club H, Harry and his posse flouted it with impunity. He had first lit up on the proverbial playing fields of Eton, and by the time he was sixteen he was regularly inhaling Marlboro Reds. A Highgrove aide dropped a dime on Harry after a weekly sweep of Club H's detritus. Although Charles detested cigarettes, he more or less forgave his son.

Unfortunately, tobacco consumption was the mere tip of Harry's acting out. Still underage, he was also a regular at the Rattlebone Inn, a Tudor-era pub six miles from Highgrove, where his older friends cheerfully bought him pints of beer with whisky chasers; or Rattlebone's specialty, the potent Pleasant Plucker cider. Afterward, an already intoxicated prince and his mates would return to Club H, where the party would continue. Although Charles had been ignorant of the excursions to the Rattlebone, he was alerted to another transgression when the distinct aroma of marijuana came wafting up from the cellar.

According to Harry's biographer Katie Nicholl, the prince first smoked pot at Eton, turned on by his older cousin and mentor Nicholas Knatchbull. Harry's parents allegedly never experimented with drugs; in fact they were strictly against them. Calling his younger son on the carpet, Charles questioned Harry's choice of friends: were they really the right circle—or posse—for a prince to surround himself with?

In the first few years after Diana's death the British press had maintained a fairly respectful distance from her sons. But Fleet Street couldn't black out reports of the underage Harry's drinking and drug use. On January 13, 2002, the *News of the World* broke the story of Harry's summer of shenanigans at the Rattlebone Inn, stating that his protection officers had been present during his after-hours drinking and toking in the pub's backroom bar, nicknamed the "magic room." More embarrassing were the reports of Harry's drunken insults of the bar's French manager, whom he'd called Froggie and addressed with another un-princely Anglo-Saxon F-word. Locals were reportedly disgusted by the prince's rudeness, muttering "little brat" under their collective breath, sharing the opinion that it was clearly inappropriate for an underage prince to be drunk as a lord and raising his voice to staff, unsupervised by the adults responsible for curbing him. And it wasn't just in his own backyard at the Rattlebone Inn. Harry, who was still in his mid-teens, was either throwing up or passing out in London's poshest watering holes on a nearly nightly basis, earning the nickname "The Sponge."

During the summer of 2001, Harry had attended the Copa de Plata polo matches in Sotogrande on the Costa del Sol, where he was spotted smoking and drinking in several of Marbella's nightclubs. Worse, he tore up a local golf course pretending it was his personal polo pitch, jockeying golf carts as if they were ponies.

It didn't seem to occur to anyone at the time—Harry least of all—that his acting out wasn't just typical adolescent wild-oat-sowing, but cries for help from a young man in deep pain.

No one listened.

So the shouting got louder.

After Charles's absentee parenting was called into question, he formed a SWAT team to convince the *News of the World* to soften the blow by running the least damaging story possible. Harry's penance consisted of an apology and a day at the Featherstone Lodge Rehabilitation Centre in Peckham, South London, where he spoke to recovering cocaine and heroin addicts. Harry was shaken by the experience but not stirred enough to sober up.

It was Camilla—whom Harry had finally been introduced to back in the early summer months of 1998, nearly a year after his mother's death—who convinced Charles that his son needed a strong father figure in his life. She encouraged her lover to be more present for both Harry and William.

Back at Eton, there was much-needed structure. Harry, like William, was keen to downplay his royal status and quick to change the subject when others tried to discuss it or make a fuss over him. He wanted to be like everyone else. Or most of all, like his mother. On Harry's eighteenth birthday, September 15, 2002, he announced, "I want to carry on the things that [my mother] didn't quite finish. I have always wanted to, but I was too young."

Where Harry was most himself, however, was in the CCF, the Combined Cadet Force. As he'd always been enamored of all things army, that was the section he signed up for. Napoleon's nemesis, the Duke of Wellington, famously declared that "the Battle of Waterloo was won on the playing fields of Eton," referencing the exemplary training of the college's generations of cadets.

In October 2002, Harry was promoted to lance corporal. He led a detachment of forty-eight fellow cadets in Eton's famous Tattoo.

Cadet Harry Wales had found a purpose.

Instead of self-destructive acting out with the Glosse Posse, the prince now devoted his weekends to leading his platoon on training exercises.

Harry had righted the ship. He took his CCF responsibilities very seriously, insisting his cadets sleep with their guns and ambushing them during night watches to make sure they were on the ball at all times. As a result of his military training and his passion both for rugby and for Eton's famously punishing "Wall Game," Harry bulked up; which, combined with his adolescent growth spurt, transformed the boy who'd arrived at Eton as a five-foot-nothing F-tit into a muscular six-footer.

He still struggled academically and had a difficult time with his A levels, the secondary school leaving qualification exams. But by then Harry had reached an important decision: he didn't need spectacular exams to get into university—because *he wasn't going.* Cadet Wales had set his sights instead on matriculating at Sandhurst, England's prestigious Royal Military Academy.

And then, as the saying goes, it all went arse over tit.

In his final year at Eton with Sandhurst within his sights, Harry returned to his indifferent attitude toward his academics, failing two of his A levels. More humiliating, his tutors demanded that he be left back, repeating the year so he could catch up.

But instead of cramming like mad for his retests, Harry sneaked off with his pal Guy Pelly to the Royal County of Berkshire Polo Club in Windsor. Speaking of arses, both teens had earned a reputation for mooning unsuspecting tourists outside Manor House—but this was a stunt on steroids.

With the prince in tow, Guy climbed to the apex of a forty-foot-high VIP tent and stripped to the buff. At that location and height, regardless of what Harry was (or wasn't) wearing, he became a security risk, as well as tabloid fodder. And the press did indeed have a field day. One front-page headline demanded to know So Harry, How's Your A-Level Revision Going? Harry's housemaster Dr. Gailey was livid. So was Prince Charles.

And yet this chain-smoking, cocktail-drinking, super-confident young man whom the press had nicknamed "Hooray Harry" had also been voted Britain's most eligible bachelor by *Harper's Bazaar.* Although the prince certainly had no shortage of giggling female admirers, he was also something of a fixer-upper.

Harry did eventually manage to get the grades for Sandhurst, but the Royal Military Academy did not accept cadets under the age of twenty; so Harry had to extend his gap year after graduating from Eton in 2003.

It was a summer of overindulgence. Harry had nearly flunked geography at Eton, but he needed no maps to find his way into countless bars and pubs from Chelsea to Mayfair to Knightsbridge, imbibing everything from beer to exotic cocktails, remaining at some watering holes long after last call. In one of them, Nam Long Le Shaker, Harry earned the dubious distinction of being able to drink three of their specialty White Panthers in quick succession. This was a delicious but potent tropical concoction served in a goblet so large it was meant to be for two.

HARRY IS OUT OF CONTROL screamed the headlines when he was photographed stumbling bleary-eyed into the night or indulging in the sort of public displays of affection with a young lady that should have been kept private.

The paparazzi bird-dogged him everywhere, even to a cattle farm in the Australian outback, where Charles sent him to cool his heels; but his antics sold papers. Harry had arrived during a republican outcry against the taxpayers being soaked for the £250,000 cost of his 24-7 protection team—a necessity, after a gate-crasher who billed himself as a "comedy terrorist" got close enough to kiss William on both cheeks during his twenty-first birthday bash a few months earlier. In New York City and Washington, DC, the horrific events of 9/11 were still open wounds, so the palace had a point; life wasn't a fairy tale anymore.

But Harry's gap year ticked on. Instead of entering Sandhurst on schedule, he would head off to explore Africa as William had done. It would change his life—but not before one more night of being caught in the flashbulbs being Harry again. This time he seemed to be emulating his uncle Andrew, photographed at the swanky disco Chinawhite with a topless model. For two years, beginning in 1981, "Randy Andy" dated the American actress/

model Kathleen "Koo" Stark. At the time, Ms. Stark was described as a "porn star" because she'd performed a steamy same-sex love scene in the 1976 feature *Emily*, then Britain's highest-grossing soft-core film.

If anyone had paused for a moment, wouldn't they have stopped to ask whether all of Harry's boozing was self-medication? And that perhaps he was dancing as fast as he could so he wouldn't feel the pain?

It was time to channel Mummy instead.

To everything there is a season, and it was a time to heal.

To CONTINUE HIS mum's charity work, accompanied by Prince Charles's head of press, Harry spent the next two months in the mountainous but tiny landlocked African kingdom of Lesotho, which means "forgotten kingdom." Lesotho has a population of two million people, but one of the highest rates of AIDS in the world. Harry and the younger brother of King Letsie III, Prince Seeiso—another second son who had tragically lost his mother when he was young—hit it off so well that they filmed a documentary together, *The Forgotten Kingdom*. The film focuses on their work at the Mants'ase Orphanage in the town of Mophato.

In Africa, Harry found his footing, especially at the orphanage. He built fences and planted shade trees. But he was particularly wonderful with the kids. Like his mum, he was unafraid to get close to children who were ill and give them a much-needed cuddle. And he'd brought rugby and soccer balls, patiently teaching games to the boys and girls, many of whom had lost parents to AIDS.

Harry fought back tears as he cradled Liketsu, a ten-month-old girl no bigger than a doll who had been raped by her stepfather. The man had AIDS and had been told by a witch doctor that having sex with a child would cure him. After Harry left Lesotho, not only did he continue to write to Liketsu's caregivers, he secretly returned to Lesotho the following September to check in on her progress.

Harry's passion and enthusiasm for the people of Lesotho and for the orphanage project were palpable. He had found his element. Moreover, he was able to put time and space between his wild child reputation and the responsible young adult he was becoming.

The people Harry met in Lesotho remained prominent in his memory after he eventually returned to the UK to commence his training at Sandhurst. Lesotho would never be a "forgotten kingdom" to him.

He had just one stopover to make first. In April 2004, Harry headed to Cape Town—the first of many such visits he would enjoy over the next half-dozen years or so—to see his current squeeze, Zimbabwe-born Chelsy Yvonne Davy. A lushly beautiful free spirit, very smart, very blond, and a year younger than Harry, Chelsy was the daughter of a safari park owner and a former Miss Coca-Cola Rhodesia. Having abandoned her early thoughts of a professional modeling career for weightier pursuits, after completing her A levels, Chelsy had quit England for the University of Cape Town, where she was studying economics, politics, and philosophy.

Chelsy was a student at Cheltenham Ladies' College near Highgrove when she was introduced to Harry by a mutual friend who was a member of his Glosse Posse. Chelsy combined golden goddess looks with the rough-and-tumble ethos of a tomboy. Harry became smitten when she told him she could ride a horse bareback and strangle a snake with her bare hands. Moreover, she was utterly unimpressed by his title: she just thought he was hot. Their physical chemistry was combustible.

In the words of Diana's friend Richard Kay, who wrote for the *Daily Mail*, Chelsy "looks sort of like an unmade bed. The passionate attraction between them fizzles and crackles. You can see they just want to rip their clothes off." Harry managed to keep his relationship with Chelsy a secret for months. The *Mail on Sunday* finally broke the story in November 2004.

But even Chelsy couldn't tame Harry. It wasn't long before the Mr. Hyde side of the prince emerged again. After a boozy evening at the London nightclub Pangaea, Harry emerged red-eyed in the wee hours of the morning, greeted by an unwelcome explosion of flashbulbs. He took a drunken swing at photographer Chris Uncle, leaving Uncle with a split lip when his own camera flew into his face. The photographer declined to press charges; but Harry's reputation, so newly on the way to rehabilitation after Lesotho, took a nose dive.

Unfortunately, he still hadn't hit the bottom.

IN JANUARY 2005, Harry and William were invited to their friend Harry Meade's twenty-second birthday party at his father's sprawling Gloucestershire estate. The theme was fancy dress (costumed, in America) "native and colonial." Dinner and champagne would be served.

What could possibly go wrong?

Prince William opted to dress as a lion, with furry paws and black leggings. Pal Guy Pelly had the *cojones* to dress as the Queen. Harry, evidently with his brother's assistance, browsed the racks of Maud's Cotswold Costumes; and with his passion for all things military, selected a sand-colored uniform, which, he reckoned, complemented his pale complexion.

The problem was, it was an Afrika Korps Nazi uniform, complete with red swastika armband.

Had Harry learned anything in his history classes at Eton? He was a military buff! Didn't he know the Nazis were the bad guys? Had he a clue about his own family's history during World War II—when his great-grandmother Elizabeth, then Queen Consort, felt proud that Buckingham Palace had been bombed because she could then look London's East Enders who had survived the Blitz in the face? Der Führer himself had called the Queen the most dangerous woman in England, because of her outspoken contempt for the Third Reich.

Why hadn't Harry's protection officers, older, seasoned, who had served their country, stepped in to say, "Perhaps Your Royal Highness might wish to select a different costume"? Didn't any of them realize that Harry in a Nazi uniform would spark a media firestorm?

Sure enough, one of the party guests snapped a photo of Harry smoking and drinking and wearing that swastika armband. The day after the party, the *Sun*'s headline read HARRY THE NAZI.

Appalling! Shameful! Grotesque! Harry was condemned by parliamentarians, World War II veterans, religious leaders and dignitaries, and, of course, Holocaust survivors and other Jewish groups. And his timing couldn't have been worse. The photos were published just six days before the sixtieth anniversary of the liberation of Auschwitz, when Harry's uncle Prince Edward would head off to Poland to represent the Queen at the commemoration ceremonies being held at the concentration camp.

Harry's blunder also conjured the unpleasant spirit of his ancestor Edward VIII, whose Nazi sympathies were known to Parliament at the time of his reign and subsequent abdication, something that older members of the royal family as well as historians would have been aware of in 2005. But even after a formal apology was issued by Clarence House, where Prince Charles resided, William privately continued to defend his kid brother's costume to their friends, insisting that Harry had only a vague idea of who Hitler was.

If true, this is perhaps the most inexcusable rationale of all, and it hardly made things okay.

Public apologies weren't going to cut it anymore. Harry had said, "I'm sorry," for his past drunken exploits, only to booze it up again. No one had any faith that this time would be different. Some members of Parliament called for his Sandhurst acceptance to be revoked. Even his grandmother thought that Harry's common sense, if he'd ever had any, had flown out the window this time.

Prince Charles, however, was copacetic with Harry's mea culpa, although he also exacted a unique punishment, banishing Harry to the Duchy of Cornwall's Home Farm to clean out the pigsties. The penance reinforced the reality that the young prince had really stepped in it this time.

THE DUCHY OF Cornwall was also about to get a duchess. The results of a YouGov poll taken at the time revealed that 65 percent of responders believed that Charles should be free to move on with his life and marry his longtime lover, Camilla Parker Bowles. This compares to only a 40 percent approval in 1998, the year after Diana died.

"Great. Go for it," Harry said when his father told him he'd proposed to Camilla. Over the past several years, both Harry and William had grown fond of Mrs. PB, as they called her. She made their father very happy; and to them, that was what mattered most.

But because Charles and Camilla were both divorced (although Charles was now widowed), the couple nonetheless had to have a civil wedding ceremony. In 2002, the church law changed with regard to divorced persons. They would henceforth be able to re-marry in the church "in certain circumstances"—leaving it up to the individual clergyperson as to whether he or she was comfortable officiating at such a ceremony. If this law had been in effect in 1955, had Princess Margaret still wished to wed Peter Townsend, she might have been able to do so in the eyes of the church, if a clergyman was willing to perform the ceremony. However, Charles and Camilla presented even more of a special situation because they had engaged in a lengthy adulterous affair prior to their divorces; and because Charles, as the future king, would also become head of the Church of England. Theirs was more akin to the situation that tripped up Edward VIII and Wallis Simpson in 1936, minus the Nazi subplot.

Charles's original intention was to have the wedding in Windsor Castle itself; but if the Queen were to grant him a license to marry Camilla there, it would transform the WC, as Prince William jokingly referred to it, into a wedding venue that *any* couple could apply for.

So Charles and Camilla opted for plan B: a civil ceremony at Windsor Guildhall, followed by a blessing from the Archbishop of Canterbury in St. George's Chapel in front of seven hundred of their nearest and dearest, capped off by an afternoon reception hosted at the castle by the Queen.

Not so fast, said Rowan Williams, then Archbishop of Canterbury. He would be willing to perform the religious blessing only if the newlyweds would publicly confess to and apologize for their mutual adultery.

Done and done. The Faustian bargain agreed to, on Saturday, April 9, 2005, after their civil ceremony in Windsor Guildhall, Charles and Camilla knelt in the transept of St. George's Chapel and openly acknowledged their "manifold sins and wickedness."

The Queen had privately given Charles her blessing to wed Camilla, but would not attend the Guildhall wedding. Although the law had been changed and she was mother of the groom, the optics would not have been good. Had she attended in her other role as Supreme Governor of the Church of England, she would be seen to condone the culmination of her son's adulterous affair. Her Majesty did, with a stony face, attend the Service of Prayer and Dedication in St. George's Chapel, and of course presided over the afternoon tea, complete with the traditional smoked salmon finger sandwiches, tarts, and tea cakes.

For years, the Queen had refused to be in the same room with Camilla—out of principle, as well as in her capacity as head of the church—and Her Majesty had never permitted herself to be photographed with Camilla. She also embargoed photographs of Harry and William with Charles's paramour. But that afternoon, the monarch finally agreed to sit for the official wedding photo of her son with the newly created Duchess of Cornwall.

# Fitting in a Box

## Acting

Having been laser-focused from childhood on the pursuit of an acting career, Meghan applied to a university that was known for its theater program as well as for its strong liberal arts curriculum. At the age of eighteen, she left sunny Southern California for the shores of Lake Michigan to attend Northwestern University in Evanston, Illinois, twelve miles north of Chicago.

Northwestern University was founded in 1855 to provide higher education to people living in the Northwest Territory. To date, the university's former and present faculty has included eleven Nobel Prize laureates, thirty-eight Pulitzer winners, sixteen Rhodes scholars, two Supreme Court justices, six MacArthur Fellows, numerous Academy Award winners, and—numbered among its equally illustrious alumni—soon to be one American-born princess.

College meant again having to navigate the sometimes confusing, sometimes insulting, sometimes humiliating terrain of being biracial, of answering the loaded question "What are you?" Meghan's first interaction with a closed-minded college dorm mate was a bit of an eye-opener.

The encounter took place during her first week at Northwestern. The girl asked Meghan if her parents were still together. "You said your mom is black and your dad is white, right?" As if that had anything to do with it.

"I smiled meekly," Meghan recollected in an article she wrote for *Elle* magazine, "waiting for what could possibly come out of her pursed lips next. 'And they're divorced?' I nodded. 'Oh, well, that makes sense.'"

Looking back on the incident years later, Meghan still didn't understand what the girl meant, even though she knew there was an implicit racist message in her words. But it had been something of a shock and Meghan had been unable to summon a reply, "scared to open this Pandora's box of discrimination, so I sat stifled, swallowing my voice."

At Northwestern, Meghan plunged herself into her studies and pledged the Kappa Kappa Gamma sorority, which was housed in a large fieldstone mansion just off campus. The venerated chapter was installed on campus in 1882.

She was back in California, home on a school break, when racism reared its ugly head again, this time with no ambiguity whatsoever. After attending a concert with her mother at the famed Hollywood Bowl amphitheater, as they were sitting in the parking lot, a driver called Doria the N-word because she wasn't pulling her silver Volvo out of her spot fast enough to the bigot's liking. Meghan had a visceral reaction to the epithet, later recalling "how hot my skin felt. How it scorched the air around me."

Her heart filled with rage and empathy as she watched her mother's dark eyes well with silent tears. "It's okay, Mommy," she said, the words coming out in a choked whisper, even as they both knew it absolutely wasn't okay. The incident had touched a nerve. Opened a wound that bled afresh. Rekindled a memory that had nothing to do with them and everything to do with them.

Just a few years earlier, Los Angeles had been ripped apart by race riots. The city was burning, sparked by the Rodney King and Reginald Denny incidents. King was a black taxi driver beaten to a pulp in 1991 by a quartet of white cops. Denny was a white truck driver attacked and beaten to a pulp by four black assailants who came to be known as the L.A. Four, after the four white cops who'd beaten Rodney King were acquitted in 1992. Meghan still remembered the ash that fell for days on parts of the city "like apocalyptic snow."

She recalled in her article for *Elle* that she "shared my mom's heartache, but I wanted us to be safe. We drove home in deafening silence, her chocolate knuckles pale from gripping the wheel so tightly."

At Northwestern, Meghan took an African American studies course, where for the first time in an academic setting she parsed the micro-prejudices of colorism—what it meant to look too light-skinned to fit in with the black community and too dark to fully assimilate into the white one.

She was also a true theater nerd and hated the possibility that someone might regard her as a cliché: one of those California girls who head east to learn how to become a serious actress. But she wanted more than an education centered around acting technique, stagecraft, and theater history classes. There had to be more; and Northwestern, being a university rather than a conservatory, offered it.

Another of Meghan's lifelong interests was politics, so she changed tracks, switching from an English major to a double major in theater and international relations.

At a school where the theater curriculum was both intense and competitive, Meghan drew high praise from her department professors. For someone who was technically still in training, being under twenty-one and still an undergraduate, she was already leaving a mark. "My lasting impression of Meghan is her sense of self," said Professor Harvey Young, who began his career as a lecturer at Northwestern in 2002 and chaired the university's Department of Theatre from 2014 to 2017.

Another of Meghan's theater professors, Head of Voice Linda Gates, remembered her in much the same way—as "being very positive. She had a very strong persona."

By her junior year, Meghan had completed most of the credits required to graduate, so she applied for an internship at the U.S. embassy in Buenos Aires, Argentina. Meghan spent the first semester of her senior year in South America. Because she had studied French in high school, when Meghan arrived in Argentina, she had no choice but to immerse herself in Spanish. It was a time of economic turmoil in the country. The peso, which for nearly a decade had been valued at 1:1 with the U.S. dollar, suddenly lost 40 percent of its value, and with it, its purchasing power.

Meghan acted as a media liaison to foreign dignitaries, an assignment in which her poise and polish as an actress, as well as her natural dignity and reserved manner, served her well, according to her half sister Samantha. The U.S. treasury secretary Paul O'Neill was in Buenos Aires at the same time; and when twenty-year-old Meghan Markle found herself riding in a motorcade of VIPs, it was heady enough to almost make her consider a career in politics.

But during a holiday break, Meghan returned home to Los Angeles. There a talent manager acquainted with one of her friends requested a copy of a student film Meghan had appeared in. After he viewed it, he convinced her she had a future on-screen and extended an offer of representation, so Meghan doubled back to her first love.

And in 2003, when Meghan received her degree in theater and international relations, she was the first member of her family to become a college graduate.

It was time to pursue her career in earnest.

While Prince Harry was running *from* photographers with his head ducked, Meghan was running *toward* them with her headshot in her hand.

At a party, a friend introduced Meghan to an agent, which led to her first few screen tests. Her first audition was for the role of Hot Girl #1, a passenger on an airplane in *A Lot Like Love* with Ashton Kutcher. She booked it. And then came the "oh, that was easy!" false sense of security from getting the job on her first try.

Because even in 2003, which was hardly ancient history, the landscape of film and television and to some extent theater casting, looked different. It's hard enough for talented people to book a job. One of the unglamorous perils and pitfalls of the business is that a performer is invariably *too* something (fat, thin, blond, tall, short, pretty, etc.) or not (fat, thin, blond, tall, short, pretty, etc.) *enough* for the part. Or else they aren't sleeping with the director/producer/star. When racial identity is thrown into the equation, it adds another *too* or *not enough* to an actor's ability to even get *seen* for some roles, particularly with unimaginative directors and casting offices.

Meghan, who had been so fussed over by soap opera divas and sitcom stars when she was a child, who had easily won the leading roles in her school plays, who had just come through an ivory tower education in one of America's finest university theater programs, and who had even snagged a bit part on a soap when she was still in college, was in for a rude awakening in the real world.

Casting directors put every performer's headshot into a categorized file, whether it's an actual one in a cabinet inside someone's office or a virtual one on the computer. Casting notices are written to describe the "types" required for every job. And Meghan didn't fit into a neat little folder. In her "ethnically ambiguous" photographs, as she put it, her looks didn't seem to check any specific box. "Was I Latina? Sephardic? Exotic Caucasian?"

The good news was that Meghan could audition for just about any role. She went on calls from music videos to commercials to feature films and series television. As Meghan described her pavement-pounding days, she had a closet full of outfits that could make her look "as racially varied as an eighties Benetton poster," depending on the call: in red she could play a Latina; in mustard yellow, she skewed African American.

The bad news was that with her brown eyes, long straight brown hair, pale skin, and freckles, casting directors couldn't "type" her. Which meant she wasn't getting any work.

Meghan discovered that she was considered too white for the black roles and too black for the white roles, "leaving me somewhere in the middle as the ethnic chameleon who couldn't book a job."

It's a truism of the business that performers are often judged by their most recent gig, and when they haven't booked one in a while, it can count against them, the unspoken assumption being *What's wrong with you?* Never mind that the competition alone among beautiful young women in their twenties is already fierce, without adding talent and connections into the mix.

As Meghan would later describe her lean years on the celebrity chat show *Entertainment Tonight*, there was a time when she was too strapped for cash to fix her car, a "beat-up, hand-me-down Ford Explorer Sport" that sounded like a "steamboat engine" when she turned the ignition. The car doors were jammed shut, so when she had to attend an audition she would have to search for a spot in a hidden corner in the rear of the parking lot and crawl over the seats to exit, then reenter, her car through the trunk. Her license plate was affixed to the rear bumper with a bungee cord and a prayer.

Like most actors and others who have chosen a career in the arts, one doesn't become an overnight sensation. Most performers would consider it a privilege just to secure steady bookings, defining a reliable paycheck as "success." Like sharks, one must keep swimming or die. *Stardom* is elusive and is achieved by less than 1 percent of the members of the Screen Actors Guild or the Actors' Equity Association.

Therefore, it's wise to have additional skills because one will inevitably end up in "survival jobs." Waiting tables. Office temping. Teaching Pilates. Tending bar. Parking cars. Meghan put all those penmanship classes in Catholic school to excellent use by becoming a freelance calligrapher. She told Matt Goulet of Esquire.com, "I've always had a propensity for getting the cursive down well," so to pay her bills while she made the rounds of auditions, Meghan was hired to hand-letter the celebrity correspondence for the luxury fashion design house Dolce & Gabbana during the busy December holiday season. "I would sit there with a little white tube sock on my hand so no hand oils got on the card. . . . I'm glad that in the land of no one seeming to appreciate a handwritten note anymore, that I can try to keep that alive." Paula Patton and Robin Thicke also tapped Meghan to do the calligraphy for their wedding invitations.

It's a skill set few have, which made it bankable; so the job was far more lucrative than busing tables and far less physically punishing. Meghan still appreciates the beauty and personal touch of a handwritten (by anyone) letter or card. Another life lesson she received from her dad was to always handwrite a thank-you note. On her lifestyle website The Tig, Meghan wrote about how excited she becomes when she receives handwritten correspondence in the mail. Years after working as a freelance calligrapher, when Meghan was a successful actress on *Suits*, she half joked during an interview that she probably still has some of her business cards floating around; and that one of these days someone will contact her to ask if she can pen the invites to their son's bar mitzvah.

It would take months to write eight hundred of them, but it would be in keeping with Meghan's personality to add that individual touch by addressing the envelopes for her own wedding invitations.

Most of Meghan's "dues paying" early in her career came in the form of walk-on parts and minor speaking roles—guest spots—on long-running television series, which most actors just call working. When she was still in college, she booked her first part—a day's work as an "Under Five" on *General Hospital*, where her father had earned a Daytime Emmy for lighting design. But a U/5 job enables a performer to secure a coveted union card; without one, it's a near impossibility to even get an audition in Hollywood.

From 2006 to 2007, Meghan appeared in thirty-four episodes as a briefcase girl on the NBC game show *Deal or No Deal*, hosted by Howie Mandel. The gig required her to hold a silver case containing anywhere from one penny to one million dollars, and to exude plenty of personality and look terrific while wearing "uncomfortable and inexpensive five-inch heels," plunging necklines, and short skirts.

It was steady employment, but it was hardly high art. Pressured not to gain any weight, the girls, among them future supermodel Chrissy Teigen, were inspected like sides of meat every morning. In order to achieve the on-screen pinup look the show's producers desired, some girls were told to pad their bras and tape their breasts, pushing them together to create the illusion of larger boobs or deeper cleavage.

Tameka Jacobs, another briefcase girl at the time, explained the daily routine to *The Express* in an interview on December 4, 2017. "[A] producer would stand on a chair and have us all line up. He'd look at us and say, 'More hair on her,' or 'Fix her boobs.'" It's doubtful that this conduct would survive the #metoo sexual harassment test today.

Ms. Jacobs also said that Meghan clearly didn't think too much of the cheesy micromini dresses the women were compelled to wear on set. "She'd be looking at you, like, 'Really?' It was clear she was thinking 'Girl, these are *short*.'"

According to Ms. Jacobs, Meghan didn't party hard with oth-

ers on *Deal* who liked to cut loose. "She always held herself high,
a princess even then."

Unlike Harry, who was still dancing like mad to erase the pain
of not having had a mummy to guide him, Meghan had a free-
spirited if traditionally strict mother to keep her on the straight
and narrow path to success. When it came to boys, Doria had
cautioned her daughter, "Honey, remember—never give the milk
away for free." While the briefcase girls were blowing off steam
for a few hours, trying to forget the humiliating way they were
earning the rent, with a producer who ogled each girl and demanded they resemble miniskirted centerfolds, Meghan's goal
was to win an Oscar or be on Broadway.

She told Esquire.com, "I would put [*Deal or No Deal*] in the
category of things I was doing while I was auditioning to try to
make ends meet." From the sublime to the ridiculous, so to speak,
"I went from working in the U.S. embassy in Argentina to ending
up on *Deal.*"

But the experience provided perspective. "It helped me to understand what I would rather be doing. So if that's a way for me to
gloss over that subject, then I will happily shift gears into something else." Meghan was tenacious and never expected instanta-
neous stardom. Her pragmatic philosophy about any endeavor,
including show business, was "Don't give it five minutes if you're
not prepared to give it five years, be kind to yourself, and Rome
wasn't built in a day."

Her career careened from a number of onetime guest spots
on popular television series like *Castle*, *90210*, and *CSI: NY*,
where she played a rich man's maid dressed in Frederick's of
Hollywood–style lingerie, to playing an FBI agent on *Fringe*, to
small roles in the big-budget features *Remember Me* and *Horrible
Bosses*. Meghan didn't even receive screen credit for her appearance in *Get Him to the Greek*.

But by this time, she was dating a man who was as ambitious as she was.

Trevor Engelson was born on October 23, 1976, in Great Neck, a tony suburb of Long Island, not far from New York City. After attending the University of Southern California, he remained in Hollywood and worked his way up in the film industry, starting out the way most aspiring directors and producers do—as a lowly production assistant. A PA's day often consists of standing around with a walkie-talkie awaiting instructions from a superior, and wrangling dozens of background actors.

Meghan and Trevor began dating in 2004. When he finally attained his dream of becoming a film producer, among his credits was the 2010 feature *Remember Me*, starring Robert Pattinson of the Harry Potter and Twilight franchises.

They had a four-day destination wedding at the Jamaica Inn in Ocho Rios, under lush palm trees, enjoying one event after another on white balustraded terraces overlooking the blue-green Caribbean. Guests played drinking games in their swimsuits on the beach the day before the vows. On 9/10/11, a mathematically popular day for many wedding couples, the duo said their "I do's" during a fifteen-minute Jewish ceremony as the sun began its plunge toward the sea. Meghan wore a simple strapless white wedding gown with a beaded gold belt; and a hundred and two of their nearest and dearest waved sparklers, while sparkling waves lapped the shore.

Afterward, everyone hit the dance floor, eager to party. Meghan and Trevor even did the celebratory chair dance, where guests hoist the bride and groom on a pair of chairs and the newlyweds "dance" in the air with a handkerchief held between them. The following morning, everyone enjoyed an al fresco brunch.

Several months before her marriage, Meghan had auditioned for an hour-long "dramedy" about a high-powered New York City law firm. Originally called *A Legal Mind*, the pilot episode would be shot with the title *Suits*. Over the course of her career, Meghan had shot five pilot episodes for TV shows that had never been picked up for production by a network. But with each pilot, there was always hope that this time the show would get off the ground and become a series.

Meghan showed up for her *Suits* audition in true California casual: a plum-colored spaghetti-strap top, black jeans, and heels, an outfit that any paralegal in a top-tier New York City law firm would be sent home for wearing, unless it was a summer Friday and the partners she worked for had all left for the Hamptons already.

However, she had a gut check right before her screen test. The character Meghan was reading for, Rachel Zane, is as smart, if not smarter, than the young associates at the law firm where she works. But because Rachel is a paralegal—who lacks a JD and is often looked down upon by those *with* law degrees—if she *thinks* like they do and knows what *they* know, then she needs to *dress* like a lawyer.

So Meghan dashed into the budget-priced retail chain H&M and spent thirty-five dollars on a little black dress without even trying it on. When she walked in for the audition, naturally the casting team wanted her to wear the dress on camera. Luckily, it fit.

The role of Rachel Zane had been conceived as the "Dream Girl—beautiful and confident, with an encyclopedic knowledge of the law." To Meghan's delight and relief, the producers weren't looking for the stereotypical Hollywood blond and blue-eyed dream girl, but simply someone who *was* the character of Rachel—no matter what the actress looked like.

Aaron Korsh, *Suits*'s creator, told *Vanity Fair* that the role of Rachel was a particular challenge to cast because it required a combination of "toughness and attitude while still being likable." After Meghan's screen test, "We all looked at each other like,

*Wow, this is the one!* I think it's because Meghan has the ability to be smart and sharp but without losing her sweetness."

She booked the job, the best role she had ever been offered.

By that time, it was Meghan's eighth year out of college, with countless rejections and near misses, the pilots that were never picked up, the onetime guest spots, the blink-and-you-miss-'em movie roles.

The day the USA Network greenlighted *Suits* "still remains one of the best days of [her] life."

True success was on the horizon.

Just when she was planning her wedding.

There are several flights a day from Los Angeles to New York and vice versa—but as it turned out, *Suits* would not be shooting primarily in New York. Instead, Toronto, which was a more difficult "commute," would double for the Big Apple.

But Trevor couldn't leave his work in L.A., and Meghan couldn't possibly turn down the role of Rachel. It was the opportunity of a lifetime. Finally she was being seen and chosen for who *she* was and what she brought to the part: her own personality and looks, and the choices she made as a performer—not as black or white or "other."

In an article for *Elle*, Meghan wrote that "*Suits* stole my heart. It's the Goldilocks of my acting career—where finally I was just right."

Perhaps it wasn't intentional: the creators selected the actress who best fit their concept of the role. Or perhaps it was intended to start conversations about a number of subjects. Rachel Zane was representative of young women in the white-collar workforce, but viewers also see her off duty, with her family, and falling in love. Selecting Meghan for the role of the brainy, sexy paralegal impacted the way popular culture defined beauty, and brought a biracial actress into the living rooms of 1.7 million households every week. Not only was Rachel a kickass role, it was a way to affect change.

Meghan got an apartment of her own in Toronto, choosing the Annex, a student enclave, instead of a more upscale neighborhood. It was in Yorkville, a tonier area, where she took her yoga classes.

With the best of intentions, Meghan assured Trevor that they would be able to visit each other "consistently." Unfortunately the long hours of *Suits*'s eight-month shooting schedule didn't allow for quick cross-country getaways.

A five-hour flight and two full-time show business careers separating them was a challenging way to start their married life. Despite the fact that they had been together for seven years prior to their wedding, their relationship had never been tested in such a way.

Meghan's passionate love scenes with costar Patrick J. Adams, an actor she had worked with many times before they were cast opposite each other again in *Suits*, wasn't what began to unravel the marriage. When an actress looks like Meghan, she'll be hired to kiss other actors on camera. And because it's Hollywood, the scripts will call for her character to disrobe, whether or not it's logical for the scene.

For Meghan and Trevor, long distance was definitely not the next best thing to being there, and instead of absence making their hearts grow fonder, they found the Toronto winters chilled them.

# Attention Must Be Paid

## Growing Up

The month after his father remarried, Harry started at Sandhurst. If there was one constant in his young life, it was Harry's fascination with the military, and that dovetailed nicely with what was expected of a male royal.

But, being Harry, he was still breaking with royal tradition. For generations, Windsor men joined the Royal Navy, including his grandfather, Prince Philip, his father, and his uncle, Prince Andrew. Harry would be the first senior royal in forty-five years to enter the Army's prestigious training facility, the Royal Military Academy.

Sandhurst was everything he wanted, but it was hardly fun. In fact, Harry said, "Nobody's really supposed to love it; it's Sandhurst . . . you get treated like a piece of dirt, to be honest."

If he made it through the eighteen-hour days of the punishing forty-eight-week training course, Harry would graduate on the same celebrated quad in front of the academy's cream-colored Georgian-style Old College as had two of the RMA's most famous alums—Winston Churchill and King Hussein of Jordan.

Harry's digs for the duration of his training were the same as every other cadet's, a nine-by-ten-foot dorm room that more closely resembled a cell with the most Spartan of furnishings: a bed, a chest of drawers, a sink, a cupboard, and a desk. Harry provided his own boot polish and ironing board. Like it or not, he was expected to press his own uniform. No personal effects were permitted; any radios had to be tuned to the BBC. The men's heads were shaved. The intention was to depersonalize the cadets and to turn them into fighting machines. For Harry, who had always wanted to blend in with the other boys, he almost got his wish. The only difference between him and the other cadets was that he received round-the-clock protection.

Sergeant Major Vince Gaunt wanted to make certain Harry had no illusions about what he was in for. "Prince Harry will call me sir. And I will call him sir. But he will be the one who means it."

Even as he conceded that he found the training challenging, Harry had found his passion. "It's a bit of a struggle, but I got through it," he would later admit. But he was *good* at it. While Harry had struggled at Eton and was at the bottom of his class there, at Sandhurst he was at the top. "I do enjoy running down a ditch full of mud, firing bullets; it's the way I am. I love it."

Popular with his mates in Alamein Company (one reason was his clandestine stash of cigarettes hidden beneath his mattress), Harry was finally excelling at something for the first time in his life.

In September 2005, on his twenty-first birthday, which he celebrated by hoisting £1.20 pints with his platoon in Sandhurst's military academy bar, Harry announced his intention to fight alongside them on the front lines. It wasn't easy to get into Sandhurst and it wasn't easy to stay there. He had no desire to be a toy soldier, and he reiterated his position to the media: "There's no way I'm going to put myself through Sandhurst and then sit on my arse back home while my boys are out fighting for their country." He took responsibility for his men as well as for his past missteps, including that decision to wear a Nazi uniform to his friend's birthday bash. "It was a very stupid thing to do and I've learned my lesson."

Harry's twenty-first birthday marked another milestone in the life of a royal. He was made a Counsellor of State, rendering him eligible to stand in for the Queen at Privy Council meetings and to represent the monarch as her emissary at official royal events.

On April 12, 2006, wearing his ceremonial No. 1 dress— dark blue tunic with white tabs on the collar, trousers with red stripes running the length of each pristinely pressed leg—bulked up, rosy cheeked, his red hair shorn, Harry and his fellow officer cadets passed out during the Sovereign's Parade at Sandhurst. The Queen herself took the salute. Harry graduated from Sandhurst with the rank of second lieutenant. His guests included Charles and Camilla and his grandparents. Also there to celebrate Harry's big day was William, who had enrolled at Sandhurst after graduating from the University of St. Andrews in Scotland. Now William was following in his younger brother's footsteps for the first time, being lower on the totem pole than the cadets in the graduating class. That meant he had to salute Harry, which Harry found tremendously amusing.

Of course Second Lieutenant Wales was the only graduate to have a granny whose role it was to inspect the troops. *Her* troops. In her beige wool coat trimmed with fur, as she slowly walked down the row of 219 officer cadets with their raised swords, the Queen stopped in front of Harry. Were his boots polished to a high shine? Did his buttons gleam? Was every red hair in place? Harry tried to suppress a grin as his grandmother and sovereign stood before him. Both of them could not have been prouder of that moment.

Her Majesty spoke to all the troops when she declared the day a "great occasion . . . this is just the end of the beginning, and many of you will deploy on operations within months or even weeks. I wish you all every success in your chosen career, my congratulations, my prayers, and my trust go with you all."

Chelsy Davy had flown in from South Africa to dance the night away with Harry at the graduation ball. A golden-skinned exotic among pasty Britons, she slayed in a figure-hugging backless turquoise silk evening gown.

Guests at a swanky American bar mitzvah would not have felt out of place at the way Sandhurst's gymnasium had been decorated for the ball. Areas were divided for various events, including a casino and several dance floors. An ice sculpture was merely a delivery system for vodka shots. Strawberries and marshmallows were on display for dipping into a chocolate fountain. Champagne was in endless supply. At the stroke of midnight, everyone gathered outdoors as fireworks spelled out *Congratulations* in the sky.

Harry had signed up to join the Blues and Royals, the second oldest regiment in the British army and part of the Household Cavalry. As the graduates removed the velvet strip from their sleeves to reveal their pips—their new officer's rank insignias—Second Lieutenant Wales learned he would now be a cornet in the Household Cavalry.

LATER THAT MONTH, Harry returned to Lesotho. He had never forgotten those who had been affected by AIDS in this "forgotten kingdom." A true son of Diana, Harry did something about it.

"I'm not going to be some person in the royal family who just finds a lame excuse to go abroad and do all sorts of sunny holidays. I've always been like this; this is my side that no one gets to see. I believe I've got a lot of my mother in me . . . and I just think she would want us to do this, me and my brother. Obviously, it's not as easy for William as it is for me. I think I've got more time on my hands to be able to help. I've always wanted to go to an AIDS country to carry on my mother's legacy."

With Lesotho's Prince Seeiso, still a dear friend, they founded

Sentebale, the Princes' Foundation for Children in Africa. Sentebale offers long-term support to Lesotho's community organizations that assist young people, especially children, whose lives have been impacted by the AIDS epidemic. In Lesotho, people use the word *sentebale* to say goodbye to each other. The word means "forget me not." That sentiment perfectly blended Harry's and Seeiso's intention of never forgetting their mothers and the charitable work they did during their lifetimes, or the children who are too often forgotten—not only by their own nation, but by so-called First World countries.

On his return to England, Harry began his twelve-week troop leader's training program at the Household Cavalry's Bovington Camp in Dorset, where he'd start to learn the necessary skills to lead a team of a dozen soldiers into a war zone. There his role would be to scout enemy positions from Scimitar armored vehicles—which meant that Harry also had to learn how to operate tanks.

While the Household Cavalry has a ceremonial presence at state occasions—a perfect way for Harry, and later William, to combine their military duties with their royal obligations—Harry had chosen this regiment for its foreign brief as well. The Household Cavalry is also charged with executing front-line recon. By the time he completed the course, Harry would be an armored reconnaissance troop leader.

Yet the party animal had not been drummed out of him, and the summer of 2006 was a particularly sodden one. William had been by his side for so much of it that the press had tagged them "The Booze Brothers," a reputation they could ill afford.

Harry spent the long summer nights of 2006 at just about every trendy venue, sometimes with William and his then-girlfriend Catherine Middleton, and sometimes with Chelsy, who was supposed to be Harry's steady girl; but on occasion, the paparazzi would catch "the spare" with his hands and/or lips where they shouldn't be, on women he wasn't seriously dating at the time. As chronicled by Harry's biographer Katie Nicholl, when the inevitable photos hit the morning papers, Harry would find himself placing an awkward long-distance call to Chelsy to explain his behavior.

To Prince Charles's relief, Chelsy was a calming influence on Harry when she was in London, but she was also enabling him: by his side in the violet lights of Boujis, a posh Kensington nightclub (and only one of Harry's usual pre-hangover hangouts), downing the famously potent Crackbaby cocktails—Chambord, vodka, and fresh passion fruit juice, topped with champagne, and served in a test tube. One night, after running up a $4,200 bar tab, Harry was photographed stumbling bleary-eyed into the night. The Queen was not amused.

Confiding in her friends in South Africa, Chelsy told them that she'd assured Harry she was in their relationship for the long haul, although she worried about her beau's roving eye. It was difficult for her to keep her word when she saw Harry in the tabloids canoodling with another woman. His infidelity was both humiliating and infuriating. Yet she also made it clear to the prince that she had no interest in becoming a member of "The Firm." According to Katie Nicholl, one of Chelsy's female friends recalled that Chelsy loved being Harry's girlfriend but "came to resent" all the outside attention that came with it. "She's actually a very private person and she hated the cameras following her all the time." She gave the relationship her best for years, but in the long run, spending the rest of her life perpetually in the public eye or constrained by centuries of protocol was not for her. Chelsy's free-spirited nature—one of the reasons Harry was so entranced by her in the first place—was also one of the reasons their relationship would go only so far.

\*    \*    \*

IN MID-AUGUST, THE Ministry of Defence confirmed that the following spring Harry would join the next regiment of Blues and Royals being shipped out to Afghanistan.

But a lot can happen in three quarters of a year.

Despite Harry's patriotism, resolve, and determination to serve, sending him to the front lines was proving to be a logistical nightmare for the MOD. For starters, corralling the media would be problematic. Even if they were not privy to sensitive information, their progress reports and updates on where the prince and his regiment would be posted compromised the troops' safety. Precious little in the world remains a secret; regardless of efforts to keep Harry's location confidential, word would eventually leak out. Because of who he was, Harry was already a target of Taliban insurgents who'd been offering bounties for his head. Centuries ago, kings and princes did lead their own troops into battle, but those days are long gone.

On the other hand, Harry had attended Sandhurst on the backs of the taxpayers at an expense of hundreds of thousands of pounds. What was it all for if he was to remain at home and never use the training he received?

Harry's uncle Andrew had felt the same way back in 1982 when he was a fighter pilot during the Falklands War—a conflict between Great Britain and Argentina over possession of two British overseas territories in the South Atlantic. At the time, Andrew was next in the line of succession behind Prince Charles.

Ultimately, the head of the British armed forces—the Queen herself—weighed in. Her Majesty supported Harry's desire for deployment to the front lines, agreeing that his military training, education, and skills should not be squandered. "She was very pro my going," Harry later said.

He arrived at his new barracks in Windsor in September 2006. Although some of his fellow officers were awed by who he was, the rank and file was made up of cooler chaps. Harry, clearly his mother's son, employed his natural empathy to put his men at ease by talking to them about their own lives and interests. They were impressed when he remembered those details.

James Wharton, who was under Harry's command then, noticed how the prince almost stripped himself of his royal position when he donned the uniform. "He becomes—even more than he should really—one of the lads," citing the way Harry would spend hours talking or playing Xbox with the guys. He really had the common touch, as Wharton observed up close. "At the time he was third in line to the throne—you can't get more aristocratic than that—but he was the most down-to-earth."

As Harry continued to train for what he hoped would be an eventual posting to the front, either in Iraq or Afghanistan, painful wounds were reopened. On December 14, 2006, the investigation into his mother's death released an 832-page document titled *The Operation Paget Inquiry Report into the Allegation of Conspiracy to Murder,* which concluded the accident was due to the negligence of a drunk driver behind the wheel. There had been no conspiracy to assassinate Diana or Dodi. In other words, it didn't have to happen. But Harry didn't have the luxury of dwelling on the events of the past or mourning what might have been. He had to focus on both the present and the future.

On the assumption that all systems would eventually be go, Harry was sent to the Castlemartin Training Area, the Ministry of Defence's 2,400-acre firing range in South Pembrokeshire, where he participated in pre-deployment exercises. He kept his nerve during simulated detonations of the IEDs, the improvised explosive devices that he would no doubt experience in country. Harry's favorite part of the pre-deployment training was known as minor agro, in which he had to get his men out of a hostile situation and fight their way out of an ambush.

An officer who trained with Harry attested to the prince's

leadership skills, his competence and confidence, and his strong and easy rapport with the soldiers. Harry also did well in cultural training, in which he was briefed on the local language and tribal customs where he might be deployed.

On February 21, 2007, Harry was informed he would be sent to Iraq that June, joining the Household Cavalry's A Squadron. The prince would carry out a normal troop commander's role, leading twelve men in four armored Scimitars.

But, Harry being Harry, there had to be a hiccup before he shipped out. A month before his send-off bash, at which he was on his best behavior, the prince had spent an evening swilling Crackbabies at Boujis with sportscaster friend and sometime flirtation Natalie Pinkham. He stepped into the night and made a lunge at an offending paparazzo, but lost his footing, ending up doing a humiliating face-plant in the gutter instead.

Unfortunately, Harry's send-off party was premature. On May 16, 2007, the Ministry of Defence slammed the brakes on Harry's deployment to Iraq. Two of the Queen's Royal Lancers had been killed there two weeks earlier. And there had been credible threats against Harry, some of which referenced plots to kidnap him and smuggle him to Iran, where it would be extremely difficult to rescue him. Sending Harry to Iraq now would expose not only the prince but those around him—a risk that had become unacceptable to the MOD. It was far too dangerous to deploy him.

Harry got it, but he was angry. However, like a well-trained royal, he stuffed his emotions in public. "I would never want to put someone else's life in danger when they have to sit next to the bullet magnet," the prince conceded after being told he wasn't going overseas after all. Friends familiar with Harry's state of mind at the time said he was emotionally gutted, devastated to the point of depression as he watched his men head off to war without him.

He'd trained with them, felt responsible for them, should have been with them. He had zero interest in being a pencil pusher in some office somewhere; and as far as he was concerned, all of his training had been a colossal waste of time, reiterating, "If I am not allowed to join my unit in a war zone, I will hand in my uniform."

The ministry got the message, although they had the final say. In May 2007, they sent Harry to Alberta, Canada, to be retrained as a battlefield air controller, learning live-fire exercises, with future plans to get him—covertly—to the front lines in that role, after the media furor over his initial plans for deployment had subsided.

The shiny object distracting them was the upcoming memorial service and charity concert that Harry and William were coproducing to commemorate the tenth anniversary of their mother's death. Assisting the princes were a number of pros from the palace, as well as from the business and theater communities.

The concert, to be held on July 1—what would have been Diana's forty-sixth birthday—and the memorial service, on August 31, the date of her passing, were intended to be upbeat; to celebrate the achievements of her young life, rather than to dwell on the tragedy of her death.

Diana's public face was only one side of her, a very small side, Harry remarked at the time, adding that he and William enjoyed their own memories of her as "just Mummy"—the blithe-spirited, music-loving mother who cracked them up with her naughty jokes and danced barefoot in their Kensington Palace drawing room to Michael Jackson's greatest hits.

As originally conceived, the July 1, 2007, concert would be a celebration for the younger generation of royals, although the twenty-three acts would include dancers from the English National Ballet, which had been one of the princess's patronages, along with pop stars from her generation—Rod Stewart and

Elton John, who had so memorably performed at her funeral—as well as icons of Charles's era (such as Tom Jones). The BBC would also broadcast the concert around the world.

To promote the Concert for Diana, which would raise money for the royals' charities, Harry and William granted their first-ever interview for American television, which aired on NBC's popular morning show *Today*. Filmed at Clarence House, where they lived with their father, the princes, casually dressed in chinos and button-down Oxford cloth shirts (Harry in pink, William in blue) were articulate, funny, approachable, and charming, completing each other's sentences.

Asked about their mother, Harry, then twenty-two, admitted that not a day went by that they didn't think of her—or what happened on the final night of her life. "For me, personally, whatever happened that night . . . in that tunnel . . . no one will ever know. I'm sure people will always think about that the whole time. I'll never stop wondering about that."

Ever since her death, Harry remained haunted by images of his mum. It was a chapter he felt would never close because "I think when she passed away . . . there was never that sort of peace and quiet for any of us. Her face was always splattered on the paper [*sic*] the whole time. Over the last ten years I personally feel as though she has been—she's always there. She's always been a constant reminder to both of us and everyone else . . . when you're being reminded about it, [it] does take a lot longer and it's a lot slower."

Because they'd never been given the time and space to breathe and grieve, ten years on, the pain of losing their mother was still palpable. Both Harry and William admitted that they knew from birth what duties were expected of them in their public lives, which is why they were always so eager for their private lives to be as normal as possible—and yet they also recognized that this ambition was a pipe dream, because there was nothing remotely normal about being a prince of the House of Windsor.

The July 1 concert was a massive success. Chelsy was there, seated in the front row beside Harry; and another 63,000 souls packed Wembley Stadium to view the event live, as it was beamed to a TV audience of nearly one billion people in 120 countries worldwide. The net proceeds of £2.5 million were distributed among Diana's favorite charities as well as to eight of the princes' charities, including Sentebale and Centrepoint—where Diana had taken them as boys to meet and chat with the young at-risk residents at the London hostel.

Harry delivered the eulogy at the memorial service for Diana, held at the Wellington Barracks on August 31, 2007. A tall, strapping man of nearly twenty-three, he seemed so far from the preadolescent boy who'd been a foot shorter a decade earlier, so somberly keeping pace alongside his longer-limbed grandfather, father, brother, and uncle Spencer—and so clearly a child then that every heart broke as he passed, his head bowed, grimly fixed on the last sight of his beloved mum, lying beneath a bier of lilies.

Time had marched on as well. There was Harry at the service proudly wearing the uniform of his Blues and Royals regiment. A slightly quivering lip was the only tell of the deep emotion he held in check as he reminded the guests of Diana's "unrivaled love of life, laughter, fun and folly," and of her importance to her sons: "She was our guardian, friend, and protector . . . quite simply the best mother in the world."

One had only to silently pause in the moment to consider some of Harry's own behavior of the past decade to recognize how sorely their protector was missed every day.

At the end of the eulogy Harry—his mother's redheaded Spencer—sat with her side of the family. The gesture was clear: Harry was every bit as much a Spencer as he was a Windsor. This memorial service marked the first time both sides of Harry's family had been in one place since they mourned his mother in Westminster Abbey a decade earlier—when his uncle Charles, the 9th Earl Spencer, eulogized Diana in a passionate indictment of the royal family, accusing them of callous insensitivity toward his sister and her unique gifts.

To everything there is a season; and now it was time to embrace.

# Uniforms

## You're in the Army Now

In short order, Harry's greatest wish was about to be granted: he was going off to war. The Ministry of Defence's Chief of the General Staff, Sir Richard Dannatt, met with representatives of both the print and broadcast media at Clarence House—off the record—to issue a D-notice, a blanket ban on media coverage until Harry was safely back on British soil. The press agreed to comply, but they had their own conditions: Fleet Street requested pre- and post-deployment interviews with the prince and access to Harry while he was in country. It was a small price to pay in exchange for his own ambitions. Harry acquiesced.

To train for his mission as a forward air controller, he spent a month at the RAF base in Leeming, North Yorkshire. In civilian terms, Harry's role would be the army's equivalent of an air traffic controller, guiding various types of aircraft, from high-speed bombers to surveillance planes to troop transport jets to supply drop carriers, to their specific targets.

On the frosty morning of December 14, 2007, Cornet Wales departed from Brize Norton air base in Oxfordshire aboard an RAF C-17 Globemaster transport jet. Coincidentally, it was the same airfield where his mother's body had arrived a decade earlier. Harry hardly traveled first class—webbing suspended from the interior sides of the plane would serve as seating for the long, bumpy flight to Kandahar. Inside his fifty-five-pound pack were an inflatable air mattress, a sleeping bag, a radio, protective goggles, sunscreen, and his favorite sweet—Haribo gummies. His weapons would be returned to him when he arrived in Afghanistan. On his wrist, Harry sported a red-and-blue Help for Heroes band. Chelsy, there to see him off and one of the few who knew where he was headed, wore an identical bracelet.

Forty-eight hours later, Harry reached FOB (forward operating base) Dwyer in the southern province of Helmand—still a Taliban stronghold, and considered one of the most dangerous regions on the planet. At the time of his arrival in December 2007, eighty-nine British soldiers had been killed in action in Afghanistan. Hundreds more had been wounded. The man who was then third in line to Britain's throne was one of 30,000 UK military personnel to have been deployed there since the start of the war in 2001.

Harry's army ID number was WA 4673A, but to the other pilots he'd be known as Window Six Seven, the radio call sign monitoring their movements. His role was to study maps and surveillance and video footage of the enemy from FOB Dwyer's operations room, in order to identify Taliban forces on the ground and verify their coordinates, so as to clear them for attack. Harry also had to coordinate with coalition air forces, because they would require his permission to enter his airspace.

No one knew who Window Six Seven was, but his posh accent made him a hit with the female pilots. He'd chat easily with them when the pressure was off and was all business when things got "hairy."

As things turned out, Harry had flown halfway across the world only to reconnect with a former grammar school classmate. His troop leader on desert sorties was an old Ludgrove mate,

Captain Leigh Dickon-Wood. The twenty-seven-year-old captain took note of Harry's easy camaraderie with "the boys," as well as the prince's ability to enjoy the rare privilege of privacy, with no paparazzi chasing him everywhere he went and no civilian protection detail shadowing his every move. Harry was in his element on the front lines, "always playing rugby or football or sitting around the fire telling stupid stories" and was a strong and competent leader when the time came.

On Christmas Eve 2007, Harry requested a particularly dangerous posting—to the Gurkhas at FOB Delhi near the Pakistan border in the town of Garmsir. The Gurkhas, or Royal Gurkha Rifles, are a unique regiment. Recruited from Nepal into the British army, the unit is particularly successful in Afghanistan because of the soldiers' ability to comprehend the nuances of the local cultures.

There was nothing left of Garmsir. Feral cats roamed its bombed-out main street. A five-hundred-yard stretch of abandoned farms, disused trenches, and the rubble from constant shelling constituted the no-man's-land that separated it from Taliban territory. FOB Delhi was subject to daily mortar attacks; it was a thirty-minute helicopter ride to medevac any wounded soldier to the closest field hospital.

In short, Harry wasn't receiving the royal treatment during his deployment. And he couldn't have been more delighted. His assignment with the Gurkhas was everything Harry wished for from a posting, everything he'd trained for. "What it's all about is being here with the guys rather than being in a room with a bunch of officers . . . it's good fun to be with a normal bunch of guys, listening to their problems, listening to what they think."

Harry spent the holiday playing touch rugby with the Gurkhas. "Not your typical Christmas. But Christmas is overrated anyway."

Whatever would his granny, whose Christmas holiday at Sandringham is considered sacred, have made of that remark?

That year, as the Queen delivered her annual Christmas Day address, which included a prayer for the safe return of every soldier on the Afghan front, only a handful of people were aware that her own grandson was among them.

Harry conceded that he had everything he could wish for: food, drink (even if the coffee and tea tasted identical), music, light, and shelter (such as it was). He and his men slept in a makeshift lean-to, made by affixing their tarps to their Spartan armored vehicle. Harry didn't even miss alcohol, he told the embedded journalist John Bingham. Or the inability to go clubbing.

"It's bizarre. I'm out here, haven't really had a shower for four days, haven't washed my clothes for a week, and everything seems completely normal. I think this is about as normal as I'm ever going to get."

When his thoughts inevitably strayed to his mother, "Hopefully she'll be proud," Harry told Bingham. "She would be looking down having a giggle about the stupid things that I've been doing, like going left when I should have gone right . . . William sent me a letter saying how proud he reckons that she would be."

Permitted only thirty minutes a week to speak with loved ones on the phone, Harry would call his family, as well as Chelsy, on the FOB's satellite phone, with its invariably spotty signal. Chelsy tried to hide her fear for his safety during their calls, keeping her end of the conversation light and upbeat, joking about how she burned yet another lasagne. Only after she hung up did she permit herself to cry.

Harry and Chelsy also Facebooked each other using aliases; and he carried her photo in his pocket, proudly telling the guys about "Chedda," his gorgeous South African girlfriend.

On New Year's Day, Harry successfully called in his first air strike after Taliban forces opened fire on a British observation post. Two F-15 fighter jets armed with 500-pound bombs were assigned to Window Six Seven within seconds. Harry guided them from six miles out to their target.

The prince would experience his first firefight on January 2, 2008. Having been dispatched with the Gurkhas for a weeklong mission to an elevated nineteenth-century fort near FOB Delhi, Harry found himself five hundred yards from enemy trenches when twenty Taliban were spotted advancing toward his location. After a Javelin missile failed to stop them, Harry took command of a .50-caliber machine gun and aimed, using the distant plumes of smoke to guide him toward his targets. Thirty exhausting minutes later, the Gurkhas emerged victorious.

But his taste of exaltation would be brief.

Unbeknownst to the warrior prince, the Commonwealth press was not being so nice when it came to obeying the MOD's D-notice on Harry's whereabouts. *New Idea*, an Australian magazine, spilled the beans in January 2008. And neither the Ministry of Defence nor Clarence House issued a denial, which was tantamount to an admission.

As a measure of damage control, during the second week of January, the six SAS (Special Air Service) soldiers who'd accompanied Harry to Afghanistan were transferred to another forward operating base, FOB Edinburgh. Meanwhile, Harry experienced his ugliest taste of war yet when a Taliban rocket intended for his vehicle struck a civilian home instead. According to one of the prince's colleagues, Deane Smith, "Harry was comforting a soldier as the charred remains of young children were removed from the battlefield to a military hospital."

Unfortunately, the MOD's efforts at containment had been unsuccessful. Ultraconservative American blogger Matt Drudge had piggybacked the *New Idea*'s article, repeating it on his website the Drudge Report. With the news of Harry's Afghan deployment all over the Internet, it wouldn't be long before he would become a deliberate target himself.

Harry was on radio duty on the morning of Leap Day, February 29, 2008, when the MOD began to receive the first reports that the prince's cover had been blown. By midday London time, General Dannatt and the Chief of the Defence Staff, a man with the Monty Pythonesque name of Sir Jock Stirrup, decided to pull the plug on Harry's deployment. It was too risky, particularly in light of his current location deep in the heart of Taliban territory.

Harry was given no advance notice of his premature departure. No explanation was provided for it. He was instructed to pack his bags immediately and say goodbye to his fellow soldiers.

On March 1, Harry arrived back at Brize Norton air base on an RAF TriStar passenger jet along with 160 troops, including three seriously wounded Royal Marines. One had lost his right leg and left arm. Another had taken shrapnel to his neck. "Those are the real heroes," Harry insisted.

And he made no secret of his desire to return to the front as soon as possible. "I don't want to sit around in Windsor. I generally don't like England much, and you know it's nice to be away from the papers and all the general shit they write."

It says a lot about Harry's thorny relationship with the press that he'd rather be a target of the Taliban than of Fleet Street and the paparazzi.

His aunt, Princess Anne, the Colonel of the Blues and Royals, awarded him a service medal on May 7, 2008. Chelsy sat proudly beside Prince Charles in a place of honor. It was her first official royal engagement. Owing to Harry's military and charitable commitments, they had seen little of each other over the past several months; and when they did reconnect, things did not always go smoothly. However, Chelsy still seemed willing to make the investment in their relationship, remaining in the UK after her law school graduation instead of returning to Africa. To that end, she had accepted a position as a trainee solicitor with the prestigious firm of Allen & Overy.

Harry was keeping several plates in the air. In the royal family, the older you get, the more demands are made on you. He and William participated in the Enduro Africa '08 motorcycle rally— an eight-day, one-thousand-mile journey in 104-degree heat to raise money for children's charities in Africa, including Sentebale, UNICEF, and the Nelson Mandela Children's Fund.

Harry was also training for his second deployment to a war zone—this time as a helicopter pilot. It would require an entirely new set of skills and rigorous exams, both physical and academic. Math had never been Harry's forte. But if he wanted to achieve his ultimate goal of flying the fixed-wing beast of his dreams, the four-blade twin-engine Apache all-weather attack helicopter, he'd have to overcome his math anxiety and manage (as some biographers have reported) his dyslexia.

Meanwhile, Chelsy was reading the handwriting on the wall and reaching her own conclusions. She had no interest in being compared to William's longtime girlfriend Catherine Middleton, whom the press had nicknamed "Waity Katie." Chelsy needed to be her own person first and foremost, and was sick of the endless loop that she and Harry were in. Everything would be wildly romantic between them; but when they were apart, whether he was in London or away at a training camp, he would flirt and canoodle with other women. She returned a blue topaz ring Harry had given her and changed her Facebook relationship status to single—a cruel, and very public, blow.

But in February 2009, when Chelsy received a copy of *Crocodile Dundee* as an anonymous Valentine's Day gift, she suspected Harry. He had always been jealous of a handsome male friend of hers from back home in Africa who literally hunted crocodiles, and he had always feared that Chelsy might hook up with him whenever things went sour. Harry denied sending the gift when Chelsy phoned to ask him ("He would say that, wouldn't he?" Chelsy told her friends); but she and the prince had such a giggle about it over the phone that it reignited their spark.

That May, having mastered the academic rigors of "heli" flying and the motor skills to pilot the smaller craft, winning the Horsa Trophy, an honor bestowed on "the man you would most want on your squadron," Harry joined his older brother at the Defence Helicopter Flying School at RAF Shawbury near Shrewsbury. The Firm should have been proud that the youngest generation was proving itself in the military. Better fly-boys than playboys. But tradition and modernity were at odds. In fact, Buckingham Palace felt the princes should be doing *more*. It was time for William and Harry to assume a larger role within the royal family, expanding their public activities.

## Moving On and Moving Out

### Suits *and Charities Abroad*

USA is the number one non-news cable network in America, and *Suits* soon rocketed to number one on its prime-time roster. Meghan's career had taken off. In 2012, during the show's second season, the character of Rachel's father, a high-powered attorney embodied by the formidable African American actor Wendell Pierce, entered the show.

Meghan believed her role on *Suits* was crucial because "some households may never have had a black person in their house as a guest or someone biracial. Well, now there are a lot of us on your TV screen and in your home with you."

However, America in particular has a fraught—and sadly, ongoing—history of racism. Some were incapable of accepting the country's biracial *president* at the time, and seeing a mixed race character on their television sets sparked an outcry. Internet trolls crawled out from under their boulders to tweet reactions that ranged from surprised ("Rachel is black?") to confused ("Why would they make her dad black? She's not black") to repulsed ("Ew, Rachel is black? I used to think she was hot"). That last comment was reported for violating the terms of use and eventually blocked, but Twitter permitted equally hurtful and racist remarks to be posted.

Meghan wrote that the comments were unexpected—yet they captured something of the zeitgeist of the times in the wake of the racial unrest of the riots in Baltimore and Ferguson, Missouri. "As a biracial woman I watch in horror as both sides of a culture I define as my own become victims of spin in the media, perpetuating stereotypes and reminding us that the States has perhaps only placed bandages over the problems that never healed at the root."

When the five-seven Meghan started booking print modeling assignments, it would frustrate her to see her freckles removed and/or her skin tone lightened by magazine editors with a heavy hand on Photoshop. The practice remained a pet peeve even after she became a star because it airbrushes her ethnicity. It was Thomas Markle who had taught his daughter to be proud of every one of her features, telling her that "a face without freckles is a night without stars," and Meghan has encouraged other young women of every race and color to embrace their natural beauty; and if they want to show it, fight for it.

Ironically, Meghan would eventually star in two television movies, *When Sparks Fly* (in 2014) and *Dater's Handbook* (in 2016) for the Hallmark Channel, the most Wonder Bread, lily-white television storyteller, playing white characters, young women with two white parents and no mention of their ethnicity in the script. But because her real mother has dreadlocks and looks black, while Meghan looks pale enough to convincingly portray Caucasian characters, she frequently heard hurtful comments about whether Doria was in fact her biological parent.

Meghan wrote in an *Elle* magazine article in 2015, "to describe something as being black and white means it is clearly defined. Yet when your ethnicity is black and white, the dichotomy is not that clear. In fact, it creates a gray area . . . a blurred line that is equal parts staggering and illuminating." She admitted being more comfortable discussing fluffier topics, such as her go-to makeup brands, her favorite scene, or her pre-Pilates rituals.

It's important to note that in her own words, Meghan Markle has "defined" herself as both black *and* white, refusing to deny the heritage of one parent or the other, each of whom not only gave her their genetics, but their life lessons and their unconditional love and support. From seventh grade, when she refused to check only one box for "ethnicity," this is proudly, fiercely, who she is. With reference to that "gray area surrounding my self-identification, keeping me with a foot on both sides of the fence, I have come to embrace that. To say who I am, to share where I'm from, to voice my pride in being a strong, confident mixed-race woman."

From now on, if Meghan had another census questionnaire to fill out, she would not do as she had done as a middle schooler. She would not even check that amorphous "other" box. "I am enough exactly as I am." Meghan's advice to her readers: *Cultivate your life with friends who don't label people by their color when they describe them but rather by who they are.* Denise in the casting department— not that Asian girl Denise who works in casting. Introduce yourselves as who *you* are, not by the color of your parents' skin. It was always so tempting when people asked her, "Who are you?" to reply that she was half Californian, half Pennsylvanian, even when she knew that wasn't the answer they were seeking.

The character of Rachel Zane was aspirational in many ways. Some of the outfits Meghan wore on camera emulated former first lady Michelle Obama's high-low mixing and matching of designer labels with more affordable brands. Meghan even wore her own jewelry on the series, including her grandmother's charm bracelet. While Rachel is usually in sheath dresses and pencil skirts with blouses or twinsets, most of those ensembles also come from top-tier fashion designers, which a real-life Rachel could never afford on her paralegal's salary. But anyone can imitate the looks for less from many chain stores, even H&M, where Meghan serendipitously pulled from the rack that thirty-five-dollar LBD that helped her win the role of a lifetime.

Unfortunately, Meghan's personal life suffered from her success. Although she and Trevor Engelson had been together for seven years prior to tying the knot, they separated in 2013 after just two years of marriage. Citing irreconcilable differences, they ended their marriage that August. Meghan didn't request a penny from Trevor in the divorce.

At the time, a mutual friend described Trevor as being "devastated at the split," adding that "suddenly [Meghan] had no time for him." It also may not have sat well with Trevor that Meghan was chilling out after a long and exhausting day on set playing Apples to Apples and drinking Scotch with the cast "into the wee hours of the night," as well as spending holidays with her *Suits* family. They shot from March through November; and Meghan, a self-described "adopted Canuck" after several seasons on the show, would join the cast for the July 1 Canada Day festivities at Patrick J. Adams's island retreat on the Georgian Bay.

But there are always at least two sides to every story, especially when the dissolution of a marriage is the plot line. Another source revealed that it was really Meghan's career that became the biggest issue between her and Trevor. "The more successful she got, the more they drifted apart." Perhaps what Trevor's ego had the most trouble handling was not the distance between Los Angeles and Toronto but a highly successful wife.

Meghan was also accepting other acting work when *Suits* was on hiatus. Even when a performer is on a successful series, nothing lasts forever. A show can always be canceled. It's safer in show business to live one's life more like Aesop's fabled ant than like his grasshopper, a steady and diligent worker when there is employment to be had; and hoarding income from one project as a hedge against lean times when work is scarce.

Meghan had a sizable supporting role in the low-budget feature *Random Encounters*, and she immediately clicked with the film's leading lady, blue-eyed blond Abby Wathen. Both women had wed at around the same time—"starter marriages," as Ms. Wathen half joked—and both were undergoing splits when *Random Encounters* was released in 2013. But while Ms. Wathen was a self-described emotional wreck, Meghan was a rock, strong enough for both of them. She refused to let a failed marriage destroy her life.

The success of *Suits,* as well as Rachel Zane's character becoming a favorite with viewers, permitted Meghan to call some of the shots in her career for the first time. Or more aptly, to refuse some of them. Speaking on a panel of women at the One Young World Summit in Dublin in 2014, Meghan discussed how she stood up to the producers. "This season, every script seemed to begin with 'Rachel enters wearing a towel.' And I said, 'Nope, not doing it.'" She phoned the show's creators to tell them, "It happened once; we've got it. We don't need to see it again." Meghan wasn't just taking a stand for herself. She was doing it for *all* actresses, pushing back against the perpetual objectification and gratuitous nudity and near nudity that has been expected of women on film for the past several decades.

Rachel became Meghan almost from the start because Meghan was Rachel—the reason she earned the role in the first place. Biracial without explanation or angst. Meghan is a foodie and a feminist. A fashionista and a fitness enthusiast. At her request, her own "foodie-ness" became part of Rachel Zane's character on *Suits.* Rachel will discuss the "crumb" of the bread during a dinner date in a restaurant, or the merits of one wine over another, just the way Meghan would. But Meghan doesn't just appreciate fine cuisine. She is a wine connoisseur and an accomplished chef—with an emphasis on organic healthy cooking.

All those years spent hovering over the craft services tables at the Columbia/Sunset Gower Studios when she was asked to avert her eyes and cover her ears because the *Married . . . with Children* dialogue was too crude for a schoolgirl paid off. "I can whip up a snack on a whim with almost nothing," and "I pride myself in figuring out how to elevate a dish with a little preserved lemon, or then a sprinkle of Maldon Salt," she told Esquire.com.

In an interview, she once described the perfect day's meals:

Breakfast: A Clean Cleanse vanilla shake blended with frozen Ontario blueberries.

Lunch: A Niçoise salad and glass of rosé, with some Grey Owl goat cheese and a baguette on the side.

Dinner: A leisurely meal of seafood and pasta, and a Negroni to cap off the night.

For special occasions, her favorite cocktails would be a spicy tequila cocktail, a Negroni cocktail, or good Scotch (neat). She then murmured, "God, do I love wine."

In early 2014, while she was filming her fourth season of *Suits*, Meghan launched a lifestyle blog, The Tig, which she described as "a hub for the discerning palate—those with a hunger for food, travel, fashion & beauty. I wanted to create a space to share all of these loves, to invite friends to share theirs as well, and to be the breeding ground for ideas and excitement—for an inspired lifestyle." The website's name was inspired by Tignanello, a full-bodied red wine that Meghan first tasted in 2007. In wine circles, it's nicknamed Tig. It was an *aha* moment for Meghan, who finally understood what oenophiles were talking about when they discussed the structure of a wine, its body, complexity, finish, and "legs."

The Tig, as a blog, is representative of Meghan getting it—in food, fashion, fitness, travel, and humanitarianism. But The Tig was "also an outlet for me personally," as Meghan characterized it, a space where she could control her own narrative and where she was able to "combat the smoke and mirrors of retouching and distortion" that were such a prevalent aspect of her life in show business, and where decisions about her physical appearance, particularly in terms of her racial identity, were often out of her hands.

It was therefore a logical fit when, in 2014, a year after her divorce from Trevor, the actress/gourmet began dating an award-winning restaurateur. Cory Vitiello, tall and handsome with a dark scruff of beard, is one of Toronto's hottest chefs in more than one sense. Vitiello, who started cooking in his parents' kitchen when he was fifteen, runs a chain of popular rotisserie chicken restaurants aptly named Flock. As their relationship heated up, he moved into Meghan's Seaton Village townhouse, where she was still residing under the surname Engelson with her two rescue dogs, Bogart and Guy.

In 2015, by then a celebrity in Toronto, thanks to *Suits*, Meghan starred as herself in a thirty-second commercial for Reitmans (pronounced "Reetmans"), Canada's largest retailer of women's apparel. It was an affectionate send-up of celebrity culture, with a dash of slapstick thrown in for good measure.

As though she's strutting a catwalk—in slow motion with a wind machine whipping her abundant hair—Meghan enters a restaurant that resembles one of the upscale locales where *Suits* lawyers might woo a well-heeled client. As she sashays toward her table, two blond female diners fangirl over her as if she's the most famous film star on the planet.

"Oh my gosh, it's Meghan Markle!" exclaims one of the women, in a stage whisper loud enough to be heard in Calgary.

"So stylish," says the other.

"I wonder what she's wearing," gushes woman number one.

Meghan nonchalantly tosses her hair to reveal the hangtag casually sticking out the back of her silky blouse. The blondes pull out a selfie stick and fall over themselves trying to get a closer look at the tag, to find out who Meghan's wearing, as the cliché goes.

She turns, catching them in the act, and says, "Ladies, it's Reitmans."

The pair of incredulous diners gasp. "Really?"

Letting the viewer in on her fashion secret, Meghan looks straight into the camera and says conspiratorially, "Really."

She was clearly having a blast.

WITH SUCCESS COMES responsibility. That's one of the tenets of Meghan's high school alma mater, Immaculate Heart. But she had always given back to her community and extended a hand to those less fortunate. She didn't need to be taught it; it was part of her ethos.

Meghan also realized that when she had a profile, it also gave her a platform. And she used it to roll up her sleeves and become involved in global and women's issues that not only were of personal interest to her but were vital to the planet.

It was in Dublin 2014, as a counsellor at the One Young World Summit, when Meghan called out the *Suits* producers for their sexism. One Young World is a UK-based charity that gathers the brightest young leaders, ages eighteen to thirty, from around the world, empowering them to make lasting connections that will result in a positive change in the world. The One Young World counsellors are "recognized leaders of integrity from around the world," who have been selected to inspire the young leaders, people like former UN Secretary-General Kofi Annan, Canada's Prime Minister Justin Trudeau, and actress Emma Watson. This summit helped launch Meghan's activism onto a global stage.

Meghan returned as a counsellor to the 2016 One Young World Summit in Ottawa. Thuli Madonsela, a South African lawyer who met Meghan at the Ottawa summit, was impressed by her dedication and commitment to the cause, as well as by "her personality, compassion, and her brain." After Meghan confided her own history with discrimination and prejudice, Ms. Madonsela better understood the actress's personal connection to One Young World and her passion for helping others navigate life's rocky shoals. "When she had this platform she thought it was her job to make it easier for other young people to discover themselves and lead their fullest life."

Meghan also became an ambassador for the World Vision Clean Water Campaign, which focuses on providing clean water and sanitation to developing nations. In 2016, writing an essay for The Tig in honor of World Water Day, March 22, Meghan admitted that she used to take long showers or let the water run while she was brushing her teeth without a second thought. From the comfort of our First World homes, we don't often think about how people live on the other side of the planet. She addressed the literal trickle-down effect that a lack of clean, potable water has on developing countries.

Outside of Kigali, Rwanda, Meghan met a thirteen-year-old named Florence who couldn't attend school because she had to spend nearly four hours every day walking to the only viable source of water—which was "riddled with germs and pesticides." Meghan also met and spoke with Florence's family. The lack of an immediate water supply robs Florence of her safety. As they walk alone on long dusty roads, Florence and girls like her are vulnerable to violence, kidnapping, and sex trafficking. The lack of access to clean water in her village prevents her from receiving an education, which steals her ability to reach her full potential.

Meghan is passionate about the ripple effect of clean water on a population, from little Florence in far off Kigali to Flint, Michigan. And while she makes a point of the importance of clean water to everyone, her focus is on women's advocacy, because women and girls are so often marginalized and still viewed as second-class citizens in so many areas of the world. Even in some of the poorest countries, while the little boys go to school, it's still the little girls who are sent to fetch the water.

Addressing an audience in New York City as part of the AOL Build series, in which celebrities are interviewed about their current projects, Meghan discussed her visits to Rwanda on behalf of World Vision, where she helped build wells so that clean water could be brought directly into the local communities. "Any opportunity to help people who have less than you will change how you move in the world. Without question I think everyone should do it," she told the AOL audience.

In 2015, Meghan addressed the UN Women's Conference as a UN Women's advocate for political participation and leadership. In a simple V-necked black top and pleated skirt, with her dark hair tucked into an elegant bun, she spoke passionately about the time her own call to action came—when she was only twelve years old and was so infuriated by the sexist television commercial that she was moved to write to Procter & Gamble and the first lady of the United States. And they listened!

Her speech focused on women's equality throughout the world:

> *Equality means that President Paul Kagame of Rwanda, whose country I recently visited as part of my learning mission with UN Women, . . . is equal to the little girl in the Gihembe refugee camp who is dreaming about being a president one day. Equality means that UN Secretary-General Ban Ki-moon is equal to the young intern at the UN who is dreaming about shaking his hand. It means that a wife . . . is equal to her husband; a sister to her brother. Not better, not worse— they are equal. . . .*
>
> *UN Women . . . has defined the year 2030 as the expiration date for gender inequality. But . . . studies show that at the current rate, the elimination of gender inequality won't be possible until 2095. . . . Women make up more than half of the world's population and potential, so it is neither just nor*

*practical for their voices, for* our *voices, to go unheard at the highest levels of decision-making.*

*The way that we change that, in my opinion, is to mobilize girls and women to see their value as leaders and to support them in these efforts. . . . Women need a seat at the table, they need an invitation to be seated there, and in some cases, where this is not available, . . . they need to create their own table. We need a global understanding that we cannot implement change effectively without women's political participation.*

*It is said that girls with dreams become women with vision. May we empower each other to carry out such vision— because it isn't enough to simply talk about equality. One must believe in it. And it isn't enough to simply believe in it. One must work at it. Let us work at it. Together. Starting now.*

When she finished her speech the UN Secretary-General led the standing ovation. And in that moment, Meghan felt: This is the point of it all: to use the status I have as an actress to make a difference in the world.

Meghan has freely acknowledged that if she did not have the high-profile role on *Suits* and a highly trafficked lifestyle website, she would not have had the humanitarian platform she'd been honored with. As she says, the hand that feeds her enables her hand to feed others. Meghan was also cognizant of the fact that while girls might be checking The Tig for fashion and makeup tips, she could also raise their awareness and social consciousness by including essays about dynamic women, some of whom they might never have heard of before. A motto she frequently posted on The Tig's banner was *Dream Bigger*. As busy as she was with her acting and humanitarian work, she still made time for The Tig. "My brain is always going. But . . . because it is all stuff that I am passionate about, it's easier not to feel exhausted as I squeeze it all in."

Two years later, on behalf of World Vision, Meghan visited the slums of Mumbai and Delhi. In January 2017, traveling under the radar, she spent a week in India. Her mission: to fight women's inequality. Meghan toured programs designed to focus on women's education, economic development, and empowerment. She learned about specific initiatives being undertaken to remove barriers to education for girls, such as building separate washrooms for female pupils and providing bicycles for girls to ride to school so they can avoid the long walks there, when they often face harassment from boys and men along the way.

At the girl empowerment groups Meghan visited, she watched self-defense classes and saw how young women were being taught to speak up for themselves in a culture that has long expected them to behave submissively; *and* to speak up for *other* girls if one of their classmates is taken out of school to be married off.

As part of a campaign to erase the shame women feel about menstruation, Meghan toured a clinic to learn more about the challenges that women and girls face when it comes to issues of hygiene and health care. She met with women and girls who have been directly impacted by their country's stigmatization surrounding menstrual health, and encountered a staggering statistic: 113 *million* girls between the ages of twelve and fourteen *in India alone* are at risk of dropping out of school because they are embarrassed to attend class when they have their periods. Without access to sanitary pads, they resort to unhygienic rags instead. They cannot participate in sports activities during their periods, and without bathrooms available for them, they end up quitting school entirely.

Another of Meghan's takeaways was that because the topic of menstruation is taboo in India, thus far there has been minimal discussion about how to solve the issue of rampant absenteeism from school, as well as the appalling dropout rate for girls. Twenty-three percent of India's adolescent girls leave school simply because they have no access to sanitary napkins and their own toilets. Enduring a quiet shame, they end up in a perpetual cycle of poverty and inequality. Deprived of an education, they also become at risk for violence and dangerous work environments, and are often forced into childhood marriage.

Meghan's goal was to learn as much as possible from the women she encountered—those living in the slums of Delhi and Mumbai, and those who were already working to improve their conditions—to see what they needed in order to be able to help them in the future.

On International Women's Day, March 8, 2017, she wrote an article for *Time* magazine about women in India and the stigma of their periods.

Now, according to Kensington Palace, Meghan will begin her married life with a fresh slate, which means a focus on different charities, likely those already under the umbrella of the foundation that Prince Harry shares with his brother and the Duchess of Cambridge. Perhaps her causes are viewed by the crown as too "political"; no member of the royal family is permitted to publicly express a political opinion. It remains to be seen whether Meghan can eventually convince the Windsors that her activism for World Vision and her other charities should be enfolded into Harry's foundation as well. After all, when each partner is an independent adult who already owns a lot of great "stuff" at the time they wed, shouldn't a healthy marriage be about combining it?

# Charities Begin at Home

In January 2009, the Queen had permitted both Harry and William to set up their own household within the St. James's Palace grounds. Their office in Colour Court was viewed as a key step toward their move into the public arena, as well as a separation from their father's household. The princes had a staff that included a press aide and their own stationery embossed with their personal crests.

Harry's charities were Sentebale; Dolen Cymru (the Wales/Lesotho connection); MapAction, which helps aid workers pinpoint where assistance is required in natural and humanitarian crises so they can reach those in need; and WellChild, an organization that provides support to ailing children and their caregivers. In order to better understand the daily challenges they face, Harry has often secretly visited ill children in their homes.

That May, to bolster Harry's bona fides as a working royal, in the midst of an economic downturn his grandmother personally financed the prince's trip to New York City for a charity polo match on Governors Island—the Veuve Clicquot Polo Classic—to raise money for Sentebale. Harry was no spectator: he captained one of the teams. Helming the opposing Black Watch team was the smolderingly handsome Argentine polo superstar Nacho Figueras, recognizable even to non-aficionados of polo as a Ralph Lauren model. Harry's Sentebale team narrowly defeated the Black Watch, 6–5, with Harry assisting in the winning goal during the final seconds of the match. The glamorous event, attended by A-list celebrities and the cream of New York City society, brought in £100,000 for Sentebale.

While Harry was in New York, he visited Ground Zero in lower Manhattan, the site of the devastating terrorist attack on September 11, 2001, where he planted a tree in the British Memorial Garden. He appeared to be the most popular Brit to visit the city since all four Beatles caused mass female pandemonium in 1964. Women screamed "Marry me, Harry!" and clamored for his autograph. One of them gushed over his "ginger hair" and proclaimed him "cuter than William."

Harry was touched by the veterans who shared their own war stories, and went to the Harlem Children's Zone, a nonprofit that assists poverty-stricken children. Giggling as hard as they were, he popped balloons with them during a relay race. Harry's mum had visited the Children's Zone during a visit to New York in 1989. When Diana cuddled a child with AIDS, it showed the world that not only was there nothing to fear about contracting the disease by hugging someone, but that everyone on earth deserved compassion. Like his mother, Harry has always been a natural with kids and they invariably return his affection with equal measures of delight.

America was wild about Harry.

His whirlwind weekend proved that just seven years after the notorious *annus horribilis*, the royal family was still as popular in America, if not more so, than it had been during Diana's heyday. If the reception Harry received in New York City was any indication, the attraction had only increased since her passing.

It was a cue to the older generation that Harry, then twenty-four, and William, twenty-six, should assume additional responsibilities. At William's age, their grandmother was already

Queen. And at twenty-six, Diana was a mother of two and ful-filling myriad royal obligations. Charles had been keen to protect his sons from the spotlight for several years—but now, despite Harry's stated wish to return to the front as a helicopter pilot, it was time for the princes to focus on earning their keep as royals.

In September 2009, the brothers combined their charitable ef-forts into the Foundation of Prince William and Prince Harry. Three years earlier, they had created the Princes' Charities Forum to team up their various philanthropic efforts. The seed money for the foundation came from a six-figure investment from the personal fortunes of both Harry and William. A third of all money raised by the foundation will go to the armed forces. The plan is for the foundation to become a grant-giving entity. After William married Catherine Middleton, as Duchess of Cambridge she became a patron as well.

Like Diana, who refused to be just a name on a letterhead and had zero interest in "fluffy" causes, Harry and William are hands-on, with sleeves rolled up, and are completely committed to *doing*, rather than being figureheads on the invitation to a char-ity luncheon or ball.

The princes also choose their own patronages—projects and charities they are passionately committed to, rather than being di-rected by the palace to become the patron of one entity or another.

In addition, Harry and William are members of the royal fam-ily's Way Ahead Group. This exclusive assemblage comprised of the highest-ranking members of the royal family and a half-dozen anonymous senior advisors was formed in 1994 to discuss The Firm's agenda for both the immediate and long-term futures. No member of government is privy to its closed-door discussions, which have included ending male primogeniture and the sover-eign's agreeing to pay income taxes.

\* \* \*

ALTHOUGH HARRY HAD made a state visit to Barbados in January 2010 to announce an annual polo match that would raise money for Sentebale, he was still clinging to his desire to remain in the army. On May 7, with Chelsy in attendance, the Prince of Wales presented his younger son with his wings. A dream had come true at last: Harry was now qualified to fly Apaches. According to a source with knowledge of Harry's character, as well as the workings of the MOD, only the top 10 percent of candidates get to fly an Apache, "and if you're heading the course, you're really an exceptional flier." Moreover, the Ministry of Defence wouldn't trust a multimillion-pound aircraft and the lives of its troops to someone just because he's a member of the royal family.

Harry's various personae were beginning to come together. As prince, soldier, and lover, he had gotten to the point where he could no longer try to sustain them individually or sequentially.

He ultimately found his niche in the military. There Harry finally seemed to fulfill his desire to be normal. His ability to relate to the average person—particularly combat veterans, as one himself—is a huge part of Harry's makeup.

He also had to blend the Windsor and the Spencer in himself. Although his mother was hardly sporty and hated "killing things" (as in woodland creatures), Harry has always enjoyed hunting and fishing on the royal estates, is an avid polo player, and throws himself headlong into physically punishing recreational sports such as rugby and football. Without his mother, he blew off steam—and grief—in self-destructive ways.

But Harry *is* his mother's son in his capacity for empathy and his compassion for those among us who have the least, especially children affected by war, poverty, and disease. To watch Prince Harry interact with a child or a group of kids is to feel your own heart melt a bit.

He has also developed a deep emotional connection to Africa.

On a return visit to Botswana with William in 2010, the princes were invited to participate in the local custom of writing down their hopes and dreams on scraps of paper. Harry's wish list included "to live in Africa," "wildlife photographer," "professional surfer," and of course, "helicopter pilot."

That year he agreed to become a cover model for *GQ* to promote an expedition to the North Pole undertaken by Walking With The Wounded, a British charity that helps injured former British armed services members make the transition from military to civilian life. A portion of the sales from every issue of that magazine would be donated to WWTW.

When the charity's founder Ed Parker half jokingly suggested that Harry, who had agreed to sponsor the expedition, might wish to join them on the arduous trek, the intrepid royal immediately and enthusiastically replied yes.

Harry trained intensively alongside the wounded warriors, learning everything that would be necessary to navigate the punishing subzero temperatures and shifting ice floes, including working with a dietician from GlaxoSmithKline who devised meals containing the proper nutrients for such an athletic undertaking in extreme conditions.

All of the warriors' belongings were packed and pulled on sleds called pulks. They carried tents, cookstoves, fuel, medical supplies, weapons, radios, and toiletries.

Liberated once again from the long shadow of his protection officers, Harry was free to be himself, to enjoy the spectacular rainbow of colors refracted through the ice that transformed the treacherous terrain into a fantastical floating fairyland.

He had to duck out of the North Pole expedition before it ended, however, for a prior engagement. Harry had always had William's back, but on April 29, 2011, he would play his most important supporting role to date.

That chilly spring morning, at exactly 10:10, William and

Harry streamed out of the driveway of Clarence House in a maroon chauffeur-driven Bentley and headed down Pall Mall past thousands of cheering well-wishers toward Westminster Abbey, where William would wed commoner Catherine Middleton. Harry, acting as William's supporter—best man, in American parlance—was dressed in the navy blue uniform of a captain of the Household Cavalry.

Filled with all the pomp and circumstance one expects of a royal wedding, it was the most glamorous and exciting event in a generation; but the night before, both princes had made an effort to be normal. Harry and William took an impromptu walkabout among the eager celebrants, members of the public from all over the world who had camped out on the Mall hoping to catch a glimpse of the wedding procession. Imagine their surprise when the flap of their tent was parted and they saw the red hair and rosy cheeks of Prince Harry, who asked if they had any drinks and snacks, and whether they minded if he joined them!

Although Catherine's maid of honor, her sister Pippa Middleton, nearly stole the show with her figure-hugging gown, and there was a great deal of speculation as to whether she and Harry might be the next royal couple, Pippa did bring a date to the wedding. Chelsy was Harry's plus one. William and Kate had been given the Queen's permission to break with decades of royal protocol by tearing up the guest list the prince's advisors had handed him, which was littered with strangers whose names he didn't recognize. Write your own list with your friends' names at the top, his granny told him. How normal!

During the reception Harry's best-man toast was warm and funny and affectionately teasing, "taking the piss" out of his big brother as he joked about William's receding hairline and the baby talk he and Kate engaged in, along with the pet names they had for each other, a dead mimic of both of them. Still, he took time to acknowledge their mother and how proud and happy she would have been on that day. William has a tough act to follow.

MEANWHILE, HARRY CONTINUED to pursue his ambition of becoming a helicopter pilot, with the hope of a second military deployment to the front lines. In February 2012, now twenty-seven, he completed his requisite sixteen months of training and was awarded the top prize for best front seat pilot, bestowed on "the student whose overall performance during the course is assessed as the best among his peer group."

Harry was also a free agent. By the New Year, he and Chelsy had split for good. As much as she loved Harry, she coveted her privacy and had never been all in for a life in the public fishbowl and the rigidity of royal protocol.

Harry threw his energy into "finishing the things" his mother "didn't get the chance to." In addition to representing the Queen on her Diamond Jubilee, he walked in Diana's footsteps, visiting Bustamante Hospital for Children in Jamaica, which had been on his mum's 1997 schedule, making his tour there particularly poignant. Ignoring his printed itinerary, Harry gave additional time to the children, speaking with them and sitting by their hospital bedsides.

Later in the day, Harry demonstrated his commitment to the Commonwealth when he utterly captivated Jamaica's Prime Minister, Portia Simpson-Miller, who was on record as supporting the removal of the Queen as Jamaica's head of state. Holding hands as they posed for a photo op, Ms. Simpson-Miller gushed about the charismatic young prince, "I'm in love with him!"

Harry then visited RISE Life Management Services, a program that provides educational and vocational support and opportunities to inner-city children. All formality was jettisoned when Harry removed his tie and, in his blue suede shoes, began dancing with the students to a reggae beat. Another dream came true when he met the widow of Bob Marley, one of his musical idols. Rita Marley presented Harry with a scarf from her husband's collection in Jamaica's national colors of green, red, black, and yellow. It would become a cherished souvenir.

On July 18, 2012, Harry attended the London premiere of the latest Batman franchise, *The Dark Knight Rises*, followed by a bit of barhopping with a stunning blonde. The following day, Fleet Street identified her as Cressida Bonas, a twenty-three-year-old bohemian beauty from a large family of artistically inclined aristocrats. Harry and Cressy had been introduced by his first cousins, the princesses Eugenie and Beatrice; and in 2010 the prince ran the London marathon with Cressy. With thirty-two of their friends, they formed a giant caterpillar, earning a *Guinness Book of World Records* mention as the largest group ever to cross the finish line in such a manner. Afterward, the group formed the Big Change, a charitable trust working for young people.

Cressy's mother, Lady Mary-Gaye Curzon, had been a cover girl during the swinging sixties, and her father, Jeffrey Bonas, is an entrepreneur, a businessman, and a historian. One of Cressy's half sisters, Isabella Anstruther-Gough-Calthorpe, now an actress, had once dated Prince William. Their grandfather is Edward Curzon, the 6th Earl Howe.

But if anyone was thinking that now was the time to engrave the royal wedding invitations, Harry got in his own way again—and in hot water with just about everyone—when he was caught behaving like a character out of the *Hangover* films.

Harry had been an ambassador for the 2012 Summer Olympic Games held in London. After the games closed in August, he jetted to Las Vegas with some of his mates for a guys' only holiday that had all the hallmarks of a Hollywood film. The lads stayed in a luxury suite in one of the newer hotels in Vegas, where every excess was indulged. There was a wet bar, a massage table, and a pool table inside the suite. Mohair padded walls masked the noise of mad carousing. The guys partied hard at nightclubs and casinos with bikini-clad go-go dancers. Harry challenged Olympian Ryan Lochte, who at that time had earned two gold medals and a pair of silvers, to a race in the hotel pool; and he invited a group of women to party upstairs in his suite.

When the ladies arrived, Harry, having lost at strip poker, was nearly starkers, playing air guitar with a pool cue and calling for a single glove so he could perform his Michael Jackson impression.

Because no one, including his protection officers, thought to confiscate mobile phones for the duration of the evening, photos of these birthday-suited shenanigans later appeared online. These days, anyone with a camera in their phone can be a paparazzo. And there was no denying that the naked guy protectively cupping the crown jewels and standing in a spooning embrace with an equally nude female reveler was Prince Harry. The giveaway was the leather string necklace that a Botswanan shaman had given to him to ward off evil spirits. It certainly had failed to protect him from all the alcoholic spirits the revelers had spent the night consuming.

In the wake of the incident, reaction was mixed—from he's representing the Queen wherever he goes, shame on him, to "everyone knows that what happens in Vegas stays in Vegas."

However, there's fun and there's conduct unbecoming anyone, least of all a member of Britain's royal family. It raised the inevitable questions of character.

But Harry assumed responsibility for his immaturity, telling CNN "I probably let myself down. It was probably a case of me being too much army and not enough prince . . . but at the end of the day I was in a private area and there should be a certain amount of privacy that one should expect."

As Harry approached his twenty-ninth birthday in 2013, his thoughts turned to settling down. In an interview for America's ABC-TV, he admitted, "I've longed for kids since I was very, very young. I'm waiting to find the right person—someone who's willing to take on the job."

The free spirits Harry had been attracted to in the past had been unwilling to make the personal sacrifices required of a royal. The Windsors are born into their duties. Their spouses must *choose* that lifestyle and understand the compromises that accompany it. It's hardly all ermine and tiaras. Most people would not trade their normal lives for nearly round-the-clock coverage of their every move, and especially in this age of social media, the constant attack from total strangers online who believe it's a valuable use of their time to criticize one's background, appearance, and loved ones.

For the time being, however, another wish was about to come to fruition. Just eight days before his birthday, Harry returned to Afghanistan for a four-and-a-half-month tour of duty in Helmand Province flying Apache helicopters. He would be based at Camp Bastion (now Camp Shorabak), at twenty-seven square miles, the largest British overseas military base built since World War II, and home to 30,000 military personnel.

Just before Christmas, while Harry was still in country, he learned that he would be an uncle. As he was no longer "the spare," now that William and Catherine's child would be third in line for the succession, Harry's destiny had changed forever.

In 2013, he increased his participation in charitable endeavors, traveling to Colorado to attend the Warrior Games, a Paralympic-style competition for wounded servicemen and women. Intrigued, Harry wanted to learn more about the games, with an eye toward producing the event in the United Kingdom. Help for Heroes and Walking With The Wounded were two of Harry's focal points now. He would eventually rejoin the brave men and women of WWTW in 2014 for their South Pole trek.

"For every life taken, which is about 450 in Afghanistan, about 4,000 are injured, and that's what we don't hear about. Arms, legs that will never grow back, as well as mental injuries. The image of your best friend being blown up next to you, that's something that will never leave you."

That August, Harry followed in his mother's footsteps to Angola, where thousands of land mines had been planted during the country's civil war, many of which remained long after the conflict had ended. One step could be lethal. Diana visited Angola during the last year of her life; a year later, in 1998, the HALO Trust was created to rid countries of land mines and make them safe for crop planting. In 2013, Harry became patron of the HALO Trust's 25th Anniversary Appeal, visiting Angola to witness the progress of the mine-clearing projects.

Meanwhile, Harry's relationship with Cressida Bonas plodded along. They attended a few weddings of friends from their social set that didn't have "no ring/no bring" rules attached to the invitations, and vacationed in Verbier, a posh Alpine ski resort, with Princesses Beatrice and Eugenie. In March 2014, after dating for almost two years, Harry and Cressy attended the first WE Day UK concert at Wembley Stadium, organized by the nonprofit charity Free the Children. You can't buy a ticket to an all-star WE Day concert. Students earn one through local and global community service.

Because it was Cressy's first official royal engagement, speculation was rife that another type of royal engagement was imminent. But the more Harry and Cressy had the opportunity to spend time together, the more they discovered that, except for their obvious physical attraction, they really didn't have that much in common. A bohemian at heart, Cressy was a former dance major at university who remained deeply interested in art and culture. In addition to her horror of the spotlight's harsh glare, she resented the intrusion of passersby snapping photos of her on their cell phones and promptly posting criticism of her hairstyle or what she was wearing.

Cressy was a beautiful girl who was being lambasted by utter strangers in real time on social media—all because she was the girlfriend of a prince. Who could handle that?

A month after the WE Day UK concert at Wembley Stadium, her amicable breakup with Harry was officially confirmed.

The year 2014 also marked Harry's final year in the army. But being normal was still high on his wish list when he said during a trip to New Zealand that he felt he needed to earn a wage and mix with ordinary people before he became a "full-time" royal.

Placing his focus on activism and humanitarian causes, that year he founded the Invictus Games, his version of the Paralympics for wounded veterans, which had been inspired by the Warrior Games he had seen in Colorado. The word *invictus* is Latin for undefeated; and the name of the international multi-sport event takes its name from the title of an 1875 poem by William Ernest Henley. The final two of the lines of "Invictus" have become the motto of the Games:

> *I am the master of my fate,*
> *I am the captain of my soul.*

Henley was an amputee himself; and the poem reflects his personal adversity and his battle with illness.

The first Games took place in March 2014, right on Harry's home turf in London. After that, a different city would host each subsequent Games, with foreign dignitaries from each participating country representing their respective teams as ambassadors, much like the Olympics.

The 2016 Invictus Games were hosted in Orlando, Florida. The Queen consented to film a cheeky promotion for her grandson's pet charity with the ambassadors for the United States team. Surrounded by American servicemen and women, President and Mrs. Obama sent a video tweet to Harry. Her arms folded across her chest, the first lady says, "Hey, Prince Harry, remember when you told us to 'bring it' at the Invictus Games?" and the president adds, "Be careful what you wish for." Their video is capped by a sneer from one soldier and a pantomimed "boom" mic drop from another.

Via the Kensington Palace Twitter account, Harry issued a reply with a winking emoji, saying, "Unfortunately for you, @FLOTUS and @POTUS, I wasn't alone when you sent me that video." Seated beside his granny on a sofa upholstered in a cheerful floral, as a fire crackles in the hearth, the prince shows her photos of a track race from the 2015 Games. The Queen is impressed. Harry receives a call on his mobile—the ringtone is "Hail to the Chief." The caller is FLOTUS. After he answers the phone, the Obamas issue their challenge, as the Queen and Harry watch the video together. Then, coyly tilting her head toward her grandson, Her Majesty smiles sweetly and says, "Boom? Really? *Please.*"

Unable to suppress a grin, Harry turns to the camera in close-up, splays his fingers, and says, "*Boom.*"

A year later, by the time the 2017 Invictus Games opened in Toronto on September 23, Harry's life was on its way to changing completely.

*Boom.* Really.

# When Harry Met Meghan

In the summer of 2016, Meghan jetted to London for a holiday. She had just returned from an ambassadorial visit to Rwanda with the World Vision Clean Water Campaign.

It was in early July that she and Harry were set up on a blind date by a mutual friend. In their interview with the BBC's Mishal Husain after the announcement of their engagement, the couple was coy about who had played Cupid. However, nothing ever remains a secret for too long. The royal matchmaker was Harry's childhood friend Violet von Westenholz, the daughter of former Olympic skier Baron Piers von Westenholz, who is close to Prince Charles. Violet and Meghan—who by that time had been part of London's social scene for a while—had crossed paths through Violet's PR work with the Ralph Lauren fashion house. When Harry, who'd long been confiding his romantic woes to Violet, told her he was having trouble finding someone, the baron's daughter replied that she might have the perfect girl for him!

According to Meghan, the only thing she had asked Ms. von Westenholz about the prince was "Is he nice?" because if he wasn't "kind," then she told her pal it wouldn't make sense for her to meet him. Although Sonia Arkadani, mother of Meghan's best friend at Immaculate Heart, recalled the girls' desire to emulate Diana's humanitarianism, during Meghan's November 27,

2017, interview with the BBC, she insisted that—unlike so many American women—she had never been a royal watcher and didn't know much about the royal family.

Harry and Meghan met for the first time in London's Greek Street, at Soho House, an exclusive membership club for creatives, with locations around the globe. At the Soho House venues, guests can stay overnight, dine, dance, exercise, relax in the spas, and avail themselves of work space, in addition to enjoying nightly entertainment. With her Every House membership, Meghan has access to the London, Toronto, and Los Angeles venues, as well as other clubs located in the United States and around the world. A house rule prohibits photographs of guests inside any of the establishments.

And although stories have been published about Harry having told a friend over drinks as far back as 2014 that his "dream girl" was "Meghan Markle from *Suits*," the prince told Ms. Husain that he had never seen the show and had not met Meghan before their blind date. It does boggle the mind, however, that Harry didn't Google her after he learned that the two of them were being set up. At the very least, who wouldn't want to know what his date looks like?

Harry said he was "beautifully surprised" when he first saw Meghan. Instantly smitten, he told himself, "Well, I'm really going to have to up my game, and sit down and make sure I've got good chat."

Their first date was for drinks, but they ended up talking late into the night. Harry said he knew Meghan was "The One" from the moment he met her.

Meghan and Harry enjoyed two dates in quick succession. Then he reportedly barraged her with text messages, hoping to see more of her. Already the pair was eagerly planning a future together, even if it was just an immediate one.

If royalty experts were predicting that the right woman for

Harry would be a combination of an aristocratic Sloane Ranger with an outdoorsy tomboy—a latter-day Tiggy Legge-Bourke, for example—then they couldn't have been paying close attention. *Charles* was the one who married his *nanny* figure, Camilla Parker Bowles having a dead-on resemblance to Mabel Anderson, the woman who gave Charles the love he didn't get from his mummy.

As for Harry, it's often been said that men marry their mothers. And if that's true of him, then from his first date with Meghan, this one was in the bag.

Maybe the stars *were* aligned. In 2015, during an interview on Canadian television in a lightning round of twenty questions, Meghan was asked, "William or Harry?" She stopped, splayed her hands, and gave the journalist a look as if it was the most ludicrous question she'd ever been asked, as if "Boxers or briefs?" would have been more logical. Finally she shrugged, laughed, and answered, "Harry."

On August 4, 2016, Meghan's thirty-fifth birthday, she posted on The Tig, "I feel so incredibly joyful right now, so grateful and content that all I could wish for is more of the same." She gave a hint about what was to come by posting under the heading *If I had one week to escape*: "I'd go completely off the grid, which I intend to do next week with some friends, some cocktails, and the sound of the lapping sea."

And some misdirection.

Just a few weeks after their fateful blind date, Harry persuaded Meghan to travel with him to Botswana. Five days in August camping together under the stars. No one but each other to talk to. No distractions, no paparazzi. In addition to Harry's presence, this was the sort of holiday that Meghan preferred—the Anthony Bourdain–esque journey of discovery to a remote corner of the world, taking the road less traveled. There in a tent beneath the sky the couple really got to know each other.

It was a huge leap of faith for both of them to jet off "to the middle of nowhere," in Harry's words, after only two dates. But both he and Meghan had an opportunity to connect and bond and test a fledgling relationship in a way that they could not have in London or Toronto. They would either get along like mad or get on each other's last nerve. What happened, of course, was that they were able to learn a lot about each other in a very short space of time.

The couple was keen to protect their privacy and preserve the fragile relationship that was blossoming, which might have been one of the reasons it survived the crucial first several months. Another reason is that Meghan and Harry are the right people for each other at the right time in their lives. In addition to their undeniable chemistry, Meghan is the first woman Harry became involved with who wants the same things he does. They both wish to change the world for the better and help young people, particularly those in developing nations, to enjoy better lives. They have both walked that walk and talked that talk for years, and both have had a platform that allows them to affect change as well. Together they can do even more, something they recognized from their first date.

In October 2016, Meghan blogged on "How to Be Both," about having a foot in two worlds: show business and humanitarian work. "To me it's less of a question of how *can* you do this, and more a question of how can you not? While my life shifts from refugee camps to red carpets I choose them both because these worlds can in fact coexist. And for me, they must." In a way, and who can say whether it even entered her mind at the time, being a member of the British royal family embraces the same paradigm. They are expected to be on all the time, and their public role as patrons of various charitable trusts, nonprofits, and foundations is very much a philanthropic one.

As royalty historian and author David Starkey phrases it, "actors, like royals, are performers. They wear funny clothes and are always on stage." And as Meghan herself has noted, as an actor she says other people's words for a living, imbuing them with nuance and subtext in order to flesh out the character she is portraying.

With regard to having a foot in two worlds, Meghan's mother once told her, "Flower, you were just born that way." Although Meghan's comment referred to the duality of the glamour of Hollywood, which is so predicated on wealth and indulgence, and her often gritty humanitarian work, she has also always had a foot in the worlds of both white and black America. She was born that way too, and has struggled against and fought back against being depicted as either/or instead of *both*.

News of the royal romance finally broke that month. The *Sunday Express* reported in October 2016 that Harry was "besotted" with Meghan and "happier than he's been in years." Less than a fortnight after the first British headlines, a royal correspondent admitted to Harry's biographer Duncan Larcombe, "We know more about Meghan after two weeks than we found out about Cressy [Bonas] in four years."

But the pair had managed to pull off a remarkable feat in this era of Twitter and 24-7 news cycles, keeping their relationship a delicious secret for nearly half a year, which allowed it time to grow organically, rather than under the media klieg lights.

Another two weeks after that, a Google search of the couple's names would yield six million hits—not all of them kind. The trolls—as well as some of the Fleet Street tabloids—were having a field day, trashing Meghan for being American and a divorcée, and for not being lily white. How dare someone from the royal family marry someone like *her*? The idiom *blue blood*, a translation of the Spanish phrase *sangre azul,* refers to the archaic notion that royalty and titled aristocrats, as opposed to the darker skinned Moors, were supposed to be so pale that one could see their blue veins pulsing beneath their skin.

Inspired by the falsehoods printed in the British tabloids, the Internet trolls crawled out of the woodwork to disparage Meghan's mother Doria, whom of course they had never met. The *Daily Mail* tagged Meghan as "(Almost) Straight Outta Compton," insisting she lived in the "gang scarred neighborhood of Crenshaw, home to the deadly street gang, the Crips." And the *Daily Star Online* announced that Harry could be marrying into "gangster royalty" because Meghan hailed from a "crime-ridden Los Angeles neighborhood." Clearly none of them knew that View Park–Windsor Hills, which has been recently listed on the National Register of Historic Places and where the median home price is $771,000, has been nicknamed the "Black Beverly Hills." To them, all black people and black neighborhoods were dangerous, criminal, and meant to be avoided at all costs. Perhaps because Meghan is an American actress and not an English aristocrat like Cressy Bonas, the gloves were taken off and she was treated as past royal *mistresses* were—as a social climber from an unsavory profession. But the added element of racism reduced the commentary to a new nadir.

In America, anyone and everyone who knew Meghan was tracked down, from friends and former classmates to neighbors and exes. Some were offered cash to spill their secrets. Even Meghan's half sister Samantha, confined to a wheelchair since 2008 as a result of MS, penned a tell-all, referring to Meghan as "Princess Pushy." Ironically, one of the Windsors has already been tagged with that sobriquet; it's the nickname most frequently given to the Queen's cousin by marriage, Princess Michael of Kent. Born in what is now the Czech Republic, Princess Michael is one of the Windsors' least liked and most controversial family members. Her father was allegedly a member of the Nazi Party, and on more than one occasion she has made tabloid headlines for her racist remarks.

As the details of Meghan's private life were being ground into an unrecognizable hash, she reportedly invited Piers Morgan, the former editor of the *Mirror*, to sit down for a drink. Perhaps, being a media-savvy woman, Meghan was attempting to gain control of her own narrative and take back her power before it was entirely wrested from her by a flock of vultures, voracious for headlines and clickbait, heedless of the truth.

Within nine days of the first story about their royal romance hitting the newsstands and the Internet, Harry had seen enough slurs and untruths being propagated about Meghan and her mother to last a hundred lifetimes.

Livid, he took an unprecedented step for a member of the royal family. On December 8, 2016, on Harry's behalf, and at his behest, Kensington Palace issued a 279-word statement to the press to back off!

> . . . *the past week has seen a line crossed. His girlfriend, Meghan Markle, has been subject to a wave of abuse and harassment. Some of this has been very public—the smear on the front page of a national newspaper; the racial undertones of comment pieces; and the outright sexism and racism of social media trolls and web article comments. Some of it has been hidden from the public—the nightly legal battles to keep defamatory stories out of papers; her mother having to struggle past photographers in order to get to her front door; the attempts of reporters and photographers to gain illegal entry to her home and the calls to police that followed; the substantial bribes offered by papers to her ex-boyfriend; the bombardment of nearly every friend, co-worker, and loved one in her life.*
>
> *Prince Harry is worried about Ms. Markle's safety and is deeply disappointed that he has not been able to protect her. It is not right that a few months into a relationship with him Ms. Markle should be subjected to such a storm. He knows commentators will say this is "the price she has to pay" and*

*that "this is all part of the game." He strongly disagrees. This is
not a game—it is her life and his. . . .*

Meghan admitted that she was hit so hard with so many mis-
truths that she made the decision not to read any of the media
coverage. She found the ugliness and racism in the press "dis-
heartening, and a shame that's the climate. But at the end of the
day I'm proud of who I am and where I come from." After making
the deliberate choice to disregard "all that noise," Meghan told
the BBC that "when you take all those extra layers away . . . it just
makes it easier to focus on being a couple."

Harry had the right to protect the woman he loves—for her
safety—and to demand a halt on the insults against her because
of the color of her skin. Any reasonable person can separate *those*
requests from asking the press not to do its job, which was how
some of the media reacted to Harry's statement. It is *never* the
press's job to defame by printing racial and sexist slurs and in-
nuendo. Harry was merely asking Fleet Street not to be liars and
stalkers.

The reaction was telling. In addition to feigning high dudgeon,
some editors got their knickers in a twist at Harry's temerity. One
called it a declaration of war, an action Harry might someday
regret. If that was this editor's view, he might wish to reflect upon
the tragic events of the night of August 30, 1997, when Harry's
mother was literally chased to her death for the sake of a story.

Other editors, including Gordon Raynor of the *Daily Telegraph*, were convinced that Harry would never have issued such
a statement if Meghan hadn't been The One. Raynor declared:
"The prince is fully aware that in issuing such a defence of his new
girlfriend and a plea to give her some space 'before any further
damage is done'—he is confirming just how serious their relationship is."

This was disingenuous. Never before had Harry been involved, seriously or otherwise, with a biracial American divorcée who also happens to be a professional actress three years his senior. And *that* was what the media was peering at under their collective microscopes.

Harry's plea failed to stop the presses. The royal romance sold papers and provided clickbait, regardless of whether the reportage was true or whether the anonymous Internet trolls combing the articles insulted both of them in the vilest terms. In England, when something as absurdly innocuous (and frankly, attractive) as being a ginger sets one up for abuse, *Meghan's* heritage was a gold mine for haters.

The racist slurs, both online and in the tabloid press, were a harsh reality check. Although Harry tried to warn Meghan about the magnitude of the attention she would receive after their relationship was made public, the couple was both surprised by and unprepared for the level of ugliness and prejudice. Harry was *born* into a life where one is in the public eye nearly every day, but Meghan would be *choosing* it. Even her status as a professional actress had thus far come nowhere near the level of scrutiny she would be enduring if she married Harry. And it would be this way for the rest of her life.

Meghan admitted that at the outset of her relationship, her parents and close friends were concerned about her. Yet they had also never seen her so happy. After Doria and her friends were finally able to meet Meghan's new boyfriend, it became obvious to them that the negative media onslaught was a temporary setback the couple would ultimately be able to transcend.

Meanwhile, Meghan continued to focus on her own profession. Far from permitting the fact that she was officially Harry's girlfriend to affect her career, she seemed to be expanding her footprint.

In November 2016, Meghan partnered with Reitmans department store in Toronto on a capsule line of workwear that might have come out of the closet of her Toronto-doubling-for-New-York-City paralegal Rachel Zane.

Discussing the collaboration, Meghan told Canada's *National Post*, "I didn't come from a world where I had access to pieces that were incredibly high-quality and expensive. Rachel Zane's wardrobe was a 'dream wardrobe' for me, and still is. Having pieces like that in my closet are pieces that I have worked really, really hard for. That's not how I have lived my life. So for me, it has always been about high-low. The other day I put up a picture on Instagram, and everyone said 'Oh my God, what are you wearing?' And okay, yes, it was a Céline bag, but it was paired with Reitmans pants, Forever 21 sunglasses, and a scarf from Zara. It's a hodgepodge because that's how we live our lives."

Meghan can be sentimental about certain items in her closet—ones that represent milestones in her life. She experienced her "Cinderella moment" in fashion when she was fitted for a Miu Miu show. The blouse and bejeweled shoes she was given to wear are archivable treasures that she is saving for a hypothetical daughter to wear someday. And if she were stranded on that proverbial desert island, the one item of clothing she would bring with her would be the *Girl Scout-o-saurus* T-shirt she wore back in the days when her mom was the leader of Troop 949 in Southern California.

When Meghan was growing up, she always headed for the department store sale rack, so she connects with shoppers who are as budget conscious as they are fashion conscious. Each of her Reitmans pieces—vegan leather pants, pencil skirt, turtleneck, bodysuit, blouse, and a faux cashmere scarf-shawl that Reitmans called a poncho—retailed for less than CAD100 (about USD78), and were personally modeled and touted by Meghan, who explained her aesthetic for the collection as "aspirational girl next door." This is Meghan Markle, the accessible celebrity, saying, "You too can dress like me for an affordable price."

Although their respective calendars were jam-packed, Harry and Meghan were clearly making time for each other during every moment Meghan had a break in her shooting schedule. In December 2016, the couple was spotted leaving a West End theater after attending the London production of *The Curious Incident of the Dog in the Night-Time.* They also shopped for a Christmas tree at London's Pines and Needles.

Little by little, Harry was introducing Meghan to his family. Rather than overwhelm them—or her—he would "try to track them down to make sure that they're around when she's popping in, without telling too many people." In January 2017, Meghan spent time with Catherine and played with her daughter, Princess Charlotte. As William and Catherine live in Kensington Palace itself, just steps from Nottingham Cottage where Harry resides, unless royal engagements precluded, it was a fairly simple matter of logistics for Meghan to get to know the Cambridges. With each subsequent trip to the UK, Meghan had been bringing more of her belongings to London, so that by February, "Nott Cott," as it's nicknamed, was more or less her home away from home.

Meghan came to know the senior royals and the other side of Harry's family, the Spencers, as well as some of Diana's friends, all of whom afforded her a deeper and fuller picture of her beau's mother. The Windsors, whom Meghan referred to as "amazing," were very welcoming, helping her, in Meghan's words, to "feel not just a part of the institution [of the monarchy], but a part of the family—which is really special." She was given solid support from the older generation, and Harry joked that "my grandparents have known [about us] for quite some time. How they haven't told anyone is a miracle in itself."

In March, Meghan accompanied Harry to Montego Bay, Jamaica, for the destination wedding of his former Eton classmate Tom "Skippy" Inskip. In his youth, Tom had been just as wild as Harry. They got up to many of their antics together, some of which involved either public nudity or illicit substances. Now, decades later, Tom was settling down, and it looked as if an altar might be in Harry's not-too-distant future as well.

Candid photos of Harry and Meghan showed them relaxed and happy and unafraid to display their obvious affection, arms about each other's waists, holding hands, gazing at each other, smiling, and laughing.

That month, Meghan began filming her seventh season of *Suits*. As her relationship with Harry was clearly serious, Aaron Korsh, the show's creator, had to consider what to do about Rachel Zane's story line. Her character arc was intrinsically linked with that of her costar Patrick J. Adams, who played her love interest Mike Ross. Adams had already expressed interest in leaving the show; so it made sense for Korsh to orchestrate a double departure, writing an ending for both actors that would permit them to leave after the seventh season wrapped its shooting schedule in November 2017.

Despite seven seasons in a principal role on a popular show, the fact that Meghan filmed in Toronto kept her pretty much under the radar for American television stars. Luckily for her, most paparazzi have no interest in slogging through a Canadian winter to log a photo of a brunette in a parka, or in dogging an actress who is not a huge household name as she discusses women's menstrual cycles in Mumbai. Meghan had never done anything outrageous or vulgar; therefore she never became a tabloid darling. People who hadn't seen her on *Suits* were largely unfamiliar with her work, either as an actress or as a humanitarian. So when the news broke of her royal engagement, there was a lot of "Meghan *Who*?" especially across the Atlantic.

Consequently, Meghan's relationship with Prince Harry thrust her into the public spotlight more than she'd ever been in all of her years on a highly successful TV series and in her philanthropic efforts combined; and she became the most Googled actress of both 2016 and 2017.

In April 2017, Meghan posted a farewell on her lifestyle blog, which seemed a clue to her followers that she was downshifting her social media presence and refocusing her priorities.

> *To all my Tig Friends*
>
> *After close to three beautiful years on this adventure with you, it's time to say goodbye to The Tig. What began as a passion project (my little engine that could) evolved into an amazing community of inspiration, support, fun and frivolity. You made my days brighter and filled this experience with so much joy. Keep finding those Tig moments of discovery, keep laughing and taking risks, and keep being "the change you wish to see in the world."*
>
> *Above all, don't ever forget your worth—as I've told you time and time again: you, my sweet friend, are enough.*
>
> *Thank you for everything.*
>
> *Xx*
>
> *Meghan Markle*

As the royal family is notoriously tight-lipped, many took it as a sign that her romance with Harry was heating up and heading toward an engagement. However, there was a far less sunny side to the fairly swift shutdown of a project that had given Meghan so much happiness. After some of the press reportedly spun information that she had shared in her blog posts into ugly and inaccurate stories about her life, Meghan believed that she was left with no alternative but to take down The Tig.

Whether Meghan had learned what didn't work from her

marriage to Trevor or whether the match simply wasn't the right one for her—or a bit of both—she and Harry made the choice to invest the time and effort necessary to make a long-distance relationship work. Despite their heavy individual professional obligations and living in different time zones, Harry and Meghan made the commitment not to spend more than two or three weeks apart. Harry took several secret trips to visit Meghan while she was in Toronto, and she flew to Britain as often as the breaks in her shooting schedule permitted. Meghan routinely had four A.M. wake-up calls on a Monday after spending the weekend with Harry. She often had to rush off a red-eye and head straight from the tarmac in Toronto to the *Suits* set.

In May, she returned to the UK to watch Harry play in two polo matches in a single day. They were spotted kissing in a parking lot after he played in the Audi Polo Challenge at the Coworth Park Polo Club near Royal Ascot, a fundraiser for two of his charities: Sentebale and WellChild. The event marked Meghan's society debut. Wearing a navy sheath dress and a white blazer, she watched the match beside the man often nicknamed "Harry's second father"—Mark Dyer—a former equerry to Prince Charles, who was instrumental in helping Harry set up the Sentebale charity in Lesotho. Nevertheless, as reported in *The Telegraph*, one of the most conservative of London dailies, "Spectators were taken aback to see Miss Markle, who made her name as an actress on the hit US television drama *Suits*, in the royal box on Saturday."

And there you have it. An *actress*.

KINGS AND PRINCES have notoriously taken the most famous actresses of their day as royal *mistresses*. Nell Gwyn was the only non-aristocrat of Charles II's numerous long-term paramours, and the only one he never ennobled. In the eighteenth century, during the reign of George III, his heir George IV fell madly in love with comedienne Mary Robinson, when he was still the teenage Prince of Wales, and promised her a fortune to give up the stage and become his lover. His younger brother, the future William IV, had ten children with the comic actress Dora Jordan. They cohabited as a happy family for two decades before George IV, then king, demanded that William dump Dora and find a bride with royal blood.

Precisely because George III's sons were forming unacceptable alliances with unsuitable commoners without the king's knowledge or consent, a law was passed to curtail the marital misbehavior of England's princes. The Royal Marriages Act 1772 forbade any royal descendant of George II, male or female, except for the issue of princesses who had already married, or might eventually marry into foreign houses, to secure the permission of the sovereign before they wed.

However, if a member of the royal family had been refused the monarch's consent and was over the age of twenty-five, he or she could give notice to the Privy Council of his or her intention to wed the person denied to them by the sovereign; and then wait a full year to marry (which is what Elizabeth II's sister Princess Margaret considered, with regard to Group Captain Peter Townsend)—unless both houses of Parliament had expressed their disapproval of the prospective spouse.

Harry's triple great-grandfather Edward VII, during his decades as Prince of Wales, and later as sovereign, numbered countless actresses and chorus girls among his conquests. But the Titian-tressed Lillie Langtry, the first official mistress of the already married "Edward the Caresser," was one of the era's great beauties. With his obvious influence, Edward helped Lillie become an international star.

Nevertheless, all of these women were looked down on as royal inamoratas, and none would ever have been considered appropriate royal *wives*.

*       *       *

AFTER THE POLO matches, Harry dashed away to attend his sister-in-law Pippa Middleton's wedding ceremony to James Matthews, then drove down to London to pick up Meghan. They headed back to Pippa's reception together. Pippa broke her strict "no ring/no bring" policy for her church wedding to make a special exception for Meghan, extending an invitation for her to attend the ceremony with Harry. But Meghan acknowledged that if she was seen entering the sanctuary with Harry, the spotlight would have been on the two of them, rather than being properly placed on the bride and groom. Instead of the headlines being about Pippa's wedding, they would have focused on whether Harry and Meghan would be next down the aisle.

With the perception that Meghan was curtailing her social media presence because she and Harry might be headed toward an engagement, all eyes were on their three-week African vacation in August 2017. After all, William had proposed to Catherine Middleton when they were in Africa, and there were several excellent reasons that Harry might do the same while he and Meghan were there. For starters, they would be celebrating Meghan's thirty-sixth birthday on August 4. They would also be visiting Botswana, which has always been close to Harry's heart, and which was where he and Meghan enjoyed their first romantic getaway. Two other idyllic adventures were planned: a safari and a spectacular helicopter ride over the 355-foot Victoria Falls on the border of Zimbabwe and Zambia that was scheduled for August 21. Royal watchers checked their calendars and speculated whether Harry might take advantage of the outstanding view to unhook his safety harness and get down on one knee as they soared over Victoria Falls.

When it didn't happen, however, most of the optimists who were avidly keeping tabs on the couple still believed that it wasn't a matter of *if*, but *when*.

Their hunches were confirmed that the royal relationship was indeed on a very serious track when Harry introduced Meghan to his grandmother on September 3. Meghan and the prince had just returned from Botswana and Zambia when Harry decided that, with the senior royals in residence at Balmoral, it would be the perfect time to zip up to Aberdeenshire, as he'd yet to pay his granny a visit all summer.

By all accounts, things went very well. "The Queen is remarkably open minded and she's very tolerant," said Sally Bedell Smith, who has written biographies of Elizabeth II, Prince Charles, and Diana, Princess of Wales. Her Majesty permitted William and Catherine Middleton to cohabit for years and had no complaint with Catherine's middle-class roots. "The Queen just looked at who Kate was and that she was in love with her grandson, and that she knew how to conduct herself with dignity and discretion, and that was the most important thing. I would imagine that the Queen's view of this would be: if they're in love and they're well suited, then they should proceed."

But if Harry had been Charles and Diana's firstborn son, would the Queen have given him her permission to marry Meghan Markle?

Has the monarchy come *that* far?

Possibly. But probably not. The stakes are different—and lower—for Harry because he becomes sixth in line for the throne after Catherine the Duchess of Cambridge bears her third child.

Before Meghan jetted off to Toronto again on September 10, she and Harry enjoyed a quiet dinner together to celebrate his thirty-third birthday a few days early.

Harry credited their reversal of the typical courtship process to its success. Because he and Meghan were flying so much under the radar, they usually spent their time at home, staying in for meals, spending cozy nights in front of the television, or inviting friends over for dinner; visiting Harry's family members for tea; and taking long country walks—instead of pub crawling or dining out all the time, where they would be constantly watched and photographed. It accelerated the process of their getting to know each other. "Slow down the dates and stay at home" became Harry's advice to the lovelorn.

He arrived in Toronto a few days before the opening of the 2017 Invictus Games and dropped by the set of *Suits*. Harry endeavored to maintain a low profile as Meghan showed him around the studio and the sets. As Harry met some of the crew and watched Meghan in action, he impressed everyone in his off-camera role of humble, proud boyfriend.

Because it was now common knowledge that Meghan was Harry's girlfriend, people expected her to be seen at the Invictus Games with him. It was only a matter of which events she might attend. That week, spectators and photographers played the equivalent of *Where's Waldo?*, looking to spot Meghan Markle in or around the Air Canada Centre.

The Games opened on the evening of September 23. Harry was in full Henry V mode as he spoke to a packed house inside the arena, rallying the troops who were about to participate in the competition:

> *Invictus is about the example to the world that all service men and women—injured or not—provide about the importance of service and duty.*
>
> *The true scale of this example was brought home to me when I left Afghanistan after my first deployment there in 2008.*
>
> *As I was waiting to board the plane, the coffin of a Danish soldier was loaded on by his friends. Once on the flight I was confronted by three British soldiers, all in induced comas, with*

*missing limbs, and wrapped in plastic. The way I viewed service and sacrifice changed forever.*

*And the direction of my life changed with it. I knew that it was my responsibility to use the great platform that I have to help the world understand and be inspired by the spirit of those who wear the uniform.*

*In a world where so many have reasons to feel cynical and apathetic, I wanted to find a way for veterans to be a beacon of light, and show us all that we have a role to play; that we all win when we respect our friends, neighbors, and communities. That's why we created Invictus. Not only to help veterans recover from their physical and mental wounds; but also to inspire people to follow their example of resilience, optimism, and service in their own lives. . . .*

*Before I close I want to speak directly to the competitors. For the next week, we entrust you with the Invictus spirit. . . . Some of you have overcome emotional challenges that until very recently would have seen you written off and ignored. And now you are here. On the world stage. Flags on your chests. Representing your countries again. Supporting your teammates. And looking up into the stands, and into the eyes of your friends and families. You are all winners. Please don't forget to love every second of it.*

*Don't forget about our friends who didn't come home from the battlefield. Don't forget those at home who still need our support.*

*And don't forget that you are proving to the world that anything is possible.*

As one of the organizers, Harry was seated amid the foreign dignitaries during the opening night of the Games. But he couldn't keep his eyes off Meghan, sitting in the adjacent section, four rows below, and looking very autumnal in her usual combination of affordable and upmarket street style—a $690 oxblood leather jacket from Mackage over an Aritzia burgundy dress that retailed for $185. Seated beside her was a close friend, Markus Anderson, the bearded publicity director of the Soho House membership clubs. Harry and Meghan had attended a Halloween party at the Toronto club in 2016.

However, others also had a bead on Meghan that night: Harry's SO14 Royalty Protection officers. Because royal girlfriends are not entitled to a protection officer, it seemed to be yet another hint that an engagement was imminent.

By this time, with the headline WILD ABOUT HARRY, Meghan was gracing the cover of *Vanity Fair*'s October issue, her freckles left untouched by the magazine's airbrushers. Her interview with Sam Kashner, which she gave shortly before she departed with Harry for their August getaway in Botswana, was published on the inside pages. "I'm going where the Wi-Fi will be weak," she told Kashner, without further elucidation. Meghan was quite open about her royal relationship, plainly admitting, "We're a couple. We're in love. I'm sure there will be a time when we will have to come forward and present ourselves and have stories to tell, but I hope what people will understand is that this is our time. This is for us. It's part of what makes us special, that it's just ours. But we're happy. Personally, I love a great love story."

The time to "come forward and present" themselves happened on Monday afternoon, September 25, 2017, when Harry and Meghan attended their first official public event together as a couple, sitting courtside at the Invictus Games wheelchair tennis match. Cameras captured them talking, laughing, touching, and holding hands. Their connection was undeniable; it was obvious from their body language, as well as the way they looked at each other, that they were very much, and very mutually, in love.

Kate Coyne, executive editor of *People* magazine, doesn't view

Meghan's romance as a Cinderella story. Speaking of Meghan as the full package—an exceptionally accomplished, poised, compassionate woman—and of the smitten way Harry looks at her—with complete love and admiration in his eyes and his heart—Coyne considers Harry to be the lucky one. "He looks at her like he can't believe he landed *her*. *She* didn't land the *prince*. *He* landed *Meghan Markle!*"

To the sartorially uninitiated, during the wheelchair tennis match Meghan appeared to be wearing just a white blouse and ripped jeans, with a caramel-hued tote slung over her shoulder.

It wasn't her outfit but the subtext that mattered. Since the dawn of time, powerful, influential women the world over, from Cleopatra to Marie Antoinette to Diana to Kate Middleton, have known that fashion is messaging. It wasn't that Meghan's ensemble screamed of conspicuous consumption. Her $185 white button-down shirt designed by her good friend Misha Nonoo is called The Husband Shirt. The $238 ripped jeans Meghan wore were made by the high-end denim brand Mother. And her $165 Italian leather Everlane purse is called the Day Market Tote. Although it's entirely possible that Meghan never gave a second thought to what she pulled out of the closet that Monday, eagle-eyed fashionistas surmised that the relationship with Harry was definitely headed to the altar.

They were right, without knowing it. On the last night of the Invictus Games, Harry and Meghan, along with Doria, enjoyed the closing ceremonies from a skybox, cheering Bruce Springsteen, Kelly Clarkson, and the rest of the entertainers performing in the concert that capped off the weeklong competition.

Harry and Meghan had held hands repeatedly throughout their appearance at the Games, usually a no-no for royal couples. And during the closing ceremonies, long lenses captured a couple of chaste kisses. However, the Invictus Games are not technically an official royal engagement and Meghan was not there in any official capacity, so she was not behaving improperly in any way. But in general, members of the royal family tend to keep their hands to themselves. William and Kate remain quite palpably in love, and it's clear when they sit together at a sporting event such as Wimbledon, that they are very much in tune with one another. Yet they still tend not to hold hands.

But in continuing to engage in public displays of affection, as well as fracturing or forgoing other royal protocols, Harry and Meghan have decided either to break with a tradition, not to care about the tradition, or to forge a new one of their own.

After the royal engagement was announced on November 27, 2017, it was revealed that during the Invictus Games, Harry had requested Doria's permission to wed her daughter.

Thomas Markle Jr. says their father was aware of Meghan's relationship with Prince Harry early on and kept their secret. He approves and gave the couple his blessing. Although the elder Mr. Markle has lived in relative seclusion since his retirement from the film and television industry and has always shunned the limelight, he has said that he would walk Meghan down the aisle, if she asked him to escort her.

Although Meghan was very close to her father when she was a little girl, by the time she was a teenager, that bond had fractured. In 2017, Ninaki Priddy, who had been one of Meghan's closest childhood friends, posted a video that she made in 1999 of eighteen-year-old Meghan. At the time it was possibly meant to serve as an amateur screen test in case Meghan ever needed footage of herself on camera. The video depicts Meghan at home in her typically teenage messy room. The bed is unmade. Family snapshots are tacked everywhere. A large brown-and-white stuffed bunny sits on one of the shelves, all of which are crammed with books and knickknacks. A Magic 8-Ball sits on her desk.

On the video, Meghan apologizes for the state of her bedroom, explaining to the viewer that she's "getting ready to move [to college]."

Cut to Meghan driving around Los Angeles in her car (*Classy Girl*—her Immaculate Heart yearbook tag—is written on the license plate holder, a gift from an ex-boyfriend) as she gives an impromptu tour of downtown Hollywood and Beverly Hills, noting the irony that at the Budget car rental location in Beverly Hills, one can rent a Mercedes or a BMW.

Then it's off to an audition for a Shakira music video. Meghan tells Ninaki that if she were to book the gig as an on-camera dancer, she'd get six hundred dollars for two days' work; but even if they selected her for background work, the job would pay two hundred dollars. To an eighteen-year-old living with her mother, who was often struggling to make ends meet, it seemed like a lot of money at the time.

After the audition, Meghan told Ninaki that it was tiring having to dance wildly for several minutes, although it was great to run into a girl she knew from doing a Tori Amos video together. With all the whatever-ism of an eighteen-year-old, Meghan didn't appear stressed out about whether or not she booked the job. But she was also about to head off to college at Northwestern; so the Shakira audition would not have changed the trajectory of her life.

As they drove home, Meghan casually remarked that she and Ninaki are "about four minutes from my dad's house." And as she continued to narrate her day in the life to her friend's video camera, Meghan added, "From my dad's house you can see the Hollywood Sign—but we're not gonna go there because we're not on the best of terms."

No further explanation was given for their estrangement, but at some point Meghan and her father appear to have reconciled. On Father's Day in 2016, Meghan posted a baby photo of herself with her dad to her Instagram feed, with the caption "Happy Father's Day, daddy. I'm still your buckaroo, and to this day your hugs are still the very best in the whole wide world . . . Thanks for my work ethic, my love of Busby Berkeley films and club sandwiches, for teaching me the importance of handwritten thank-you notes and for giving me that signature Markle nose. I love you xo—Bean."

Although Thomas Markle still maintains a very modest pied-à-terre in Los Angeles, he currently lives in Rosarito Beach, Mexico, among other American expats. He earned an excellent salary as a Hollywood lighting designer and director of photography, but his retirement years have not been kind. He was compelled to file for bankruptcy in 2016, allegedly due to a business deal that went sour. According to Thomas Markle Jr., his son from his first marriage, their father never had another serious relationship with a woman after he and Doria were divorced.

As of November 2017, Harry had spoken with Meghan's father a few times, but the men had yet to meet in person.

However, there was only one relative on either side whose blessing was *legally* required. A residual of the Royal Marriages Act 1772 remains in effect; and as such, Harry needed the monarch's consent to wed Meghan Markle. This act was repealed on March 26, 2015, to apply only to the first six people in the line of succession. As Harry was fifth in line toward the end of 2017 when he requested his grandmother's permission to marry Meghan, the act still applied to him. George III never could have imagined that 245 years after he acquired a legal remedy to prevent his sons from marrying actresses, that one of his descendants would seek the sovereign's approval to do just that.

In October 2017, shortly after it was announced that Meghan would not be returning to the cast of *Suits*, she made her first visit to Buckingham Palace to take tea with Her Majesty. It was, Meghan said, "an incredible experience" to get to know the Queen "through [Harry's] lens—not just through his honor and respect for her as the monarch, but the love that he has for her as his grandmother. All of those layers have been so important for me. So when I met her, I had such a deep understanding; and of course, an incredible respect for being able to have that time with her. And she's an incredible woman."

Evidently the canine members of the royal family enthusiastically approved of Meghan from the start. "The corgis took to her straightaway," Harry enthused. "For the last thirty-three years I've been barked at. This one walks in: absolutely nothing."

Meghan chuckled. "They were just laying on my feet during tea."

"Wagging their tails," Harry added, wagging his right hand for emphasis.

Meghan and Harry display an ease in each other's presence that combines the flush of new love with the complete sense of trust often displayed by couples who have been together for a long time. They hold hands, will give each other a reassuring touch on the back, and make frequent eye contact, sharing a gaze that brims with love. It's more than smitten; there's depth behind it.

One of the ways that Meghan has shown that *she's* also got *Harry's* back has been her encouragement and support of his speaking publicly about his decision to seek the professional counseling that would enable him to finally process his mother's death.

Harry and William had never been permitted the opportunity to fully and properly mourn their mum. Their duty is to serve the institution of the monarchy and to be resilient for the sake of their subjects, the rationale being that if the members of the royal family are seen to be in puddles of tears, the populace might lose its famous British will to Keep Calm and Carry On. As Harry had mentioned ten years after his mother's passing, with her face all over the media, it was impossible to move forward in a healthy way. It's no wonder that a twelve-year-old boy lost his footing, with his father focused on Camilla and hired protection officers serving in loco parentis. Because Harry was expected to stuff his grief, his wildness and his drug and alcohol use as a minor, even his slugging of paparazzi, who represented her "murderers"—although he wasn't aware of it at the time—were his unhealthy and ultimately self-destructive methods of coping with the daily pain.

In October 2017, Harry joined William and Catherine to partner with the nonprofit organization Heads Together, working to help eliminate the stigma surrounding mental health. In April, Harry had disclosed to *The Telegraph* that he was twenty-eight years old when he made the decision to speak to a mental health professional. Harry had "shut down all his emotions" after his mother died, spending nearly twenty years of hell "trying not to think about" her death, "followed by two years of chaos."

He'd granted a rare interview that month with Bryony Gordon for her podcast Mad World. Although he admitted to being a bit nervous at first, Harry spent thirty minutes candidly discussing this dark period of his life, in the hope that his ability to get to a better place emotionally and psychologically after professional counseling would destigmatize the issue of mental health and inspire others to seek help. He even described taking up boxing as a healthier outlet for working out his aggression. "And that really saved me, because being able to punch someone who was wearing pads was certainly easier."

Losing his mother had a "serious effect" on Harry's personal and professional life. Being so much in the public eye, he was often on the verge of a nervous breakdown, "when all sorts of grief and sorts of lies and misconceptions and everything are coming to you from every angle." For years he suffered a fight-or-flight reaction during public engagements. Harry had perennially stuck his head in the sand, refusing to think about his mother, "because why would that help? I thought, 'It's only going to make you sad. It's not going to bring her back.'"

Harry admitted that it took William and others who were close to him, including Meghan, whose name he did not reveal during the interview, to tell him, "Look, you really need to deal with this. It is not normal to think that nothing has affected you."

The sense of relief Harry felt after unburdening himself and finally being able to speak honestly about his feelings was a revelation. After undergoing therapy he finally felt able to put the "blood, sweat, and tears" into making a difference for others. The angry young man had learned to mourn his mother in a way that was no longer self-destructive.

Working with Heads Together, Harry aims to normalize the conversation so that anyone, male or female, can sit down with someone else over a cup of coffee and just admit to that person, "I've had a sh*tty day; can I just tell you about it?" Speaking to American journalist Robin Roberts on ABC Television's *Nightline*, Harry said, "Everybody needs a hug every now and then, and it just so happens I've been told over and over again that I'm very good with hugs, which is great, good at giving them—fantastic." Because after people let it all out, they can just walk away and be in a much better place emotionally.

While Harry is quick to say that his mental health issues stemmed from the inability to process his grief, and not from PTSD after returning from Afghanistan, he did work with the army's personnel recovery unit; and the experience of listening to wounded servicemen and servicewomen discussing their own psychological and emotional traumas ended up becoming a catalyst in his own understanding of the importance of opening up.

"I know there is huge merit in talking about your issues and the only thing about keeping it quiet is that it's only ever going to make it worse. Not just for you but for everybody else around you as well, because you become a problem. I, through a lot of my twenties, was a problem, and I didn't know how to deal with it."

What Harry discovered as he began seeking counseling was that "once you start talking about it, you realize you're part of quite a big club. I can't encourage people enough to have this conversation because you will be surprised, firstly, how much support you get, and secondly, how many people literally are longing for you to come out."

A dam had burst. Harry also spoke to *Newsweek* about his journey toward mental health. "My search began when I was in my mid-twenties. I needed to fix the mistakes I was making. . . . I didn't want to be in the position I was in, but eventually I pulled my head out of the sand, started listening to people and decided to use my role for good."

# Harry Hitches His Wagon to a Star

As soon as she wrapped her final season of *Suits*, Meghan left Toronto and moved in permanently with Harry. Before she met the prince, the two loves of her life were without a doubt her rescue dogs Bogart and Guy, who made numerous guest appearances on her Instagram feed. Guy made the trip across the pond, but Bogart was reportedly too old to fly safely across the Atlantic. It was a sad parting for both of them but the beginning of a beautiful friendship in Bogart's new forever home with dear friends of Meghan's in Southern California.

Having begun her Toronto life in the student district, after *Suits* took off, Meghan had rented a two-story home with a front porch and a backyard on Yarmouth Road in the Seaton Village neighborhood, where the average home price is over a million dollars. She made the decor as Southern Californian as she could by exposing the hardwood floors and letting in as much light as possible in order to avoid becoming homesick during those cold Canadian winters. Harry visited Meghan here as often as his schedule permitted. After she moved to London, the owners put the Seaton Village house on the market for just under $1.4 million.

Meghan also began scouting properties in London so that her family would have a pied-à-terre when they came to visit. She and Harry reside on the Kensington Palace grounds in the

1,324-square foot Nottingham Cottage. It's the smallest separate residence on the seventeenth-century estate, but its charm factor can't be beat. William and Kate lived there when they were first married. At that time, Harry resided in Kensington Palace's Apartment 4B, a little grace and favor unit that had only one bedroom, one bath, a sitting room, and a kitchen.

In 2016, following extensive renovations, the Cambridges and their children moved into the twenty-one-room Apartment 1A in Kensington Palace, making it their permanent residence in 2017; and Harry took over "Nott Cott."

A Realtor would describe the cottage as "cozy and private." In an old photo taken by a previous tenant of Apartment 1A, the late Princess Margaret's husband Lord Snowdon, the rosebushes are so lush and abundant that they nearly threaten to envelop the home's first story. Surrounded by a white picket fence, the brick cottage features two bedrooms, a pair of reception rooms, and only one bathroom, but it has a small yard where Meghan's rescue beagle, Guy, can romp to his little heart's content.

Like much of the Kensington Palace grounds, Nottingham Cottage claims a historic lineage. It was designed by Sir Christopher Wren, better known for loftier edifices, including St. Paul's Cathedral. Naturally, Nott Cott doesn't boast the soaring interiors of St. Paul's. Evidently, when Prince William, who is six-three, lived there, he had to duck to avoid hitting his head as he entered. Another previous tenant of Nott Cott was Harry's aunt, Diana's sister Lady Jane Fellowes, who was married to Her Majesty's former secretary Robert Fellowes.

In early November 2017, Harry proposed to Meghan in Nottingham Cottage. They were enjoying a routine evening in, "trying to roast a chicken," when Harry popped the question that Meghan—and everyone who had been following their romance—had been eagerly anticipating.

Meghan had once told *Good Housekeeping* magazine, "There's nothing as delicious (or as impressive) as a perfectly roasted chicken. It's a game changer," and there isn't a person on Planet Earth who would quibble with that assessment. Meghan's recipe reportedly comes from Ina Garten, the celebrity chef from East Hampton, New York, known as the Barefoot Contessa. Called the Perfect Roast Chicken, this beginner-level recipe that landed a prince can be found online.

About three weeks later, on November 27, the Prince of Wales released the official announcement from Clarence House.

### HIS ROYAL HIGHNESS PRINCE HENRY OF WALES AND MISS MEGHAN MARKLE ARE ENGAGED TO BE MARRIED

His Royal Highness The Prince of Wales is delighted to announce the engagement of Prince Harry to Ms. Meghan Markle.

The wedding will take place in Spring 2018. Further details about the wedding day will take place in due course.

His Royal Highness and Ms. Markle became engaged in London earlier this month. Prince Harry has informed Her Majesty The Queen and other close members of his family. Prince Harry has also sought and received the blessing of Ms. Markle's parents.

The couple will live at Nottingham Cottage at Kensington Palace.

Kensington Palace also released a statement from Meghan's parents on official letterhead below Harry's crest that read:

On the announcement of their daughter Meghan Markle's engagement to His Royal Highness Prince Henry of Wales, Mr. Thomas Markle and Mrs. Doria Ragland said:

"We are incredibly happy for Meghan and Harry. Our daughter has always been a kind and loving person. To see her union with Harry, who shares the same qualities, is a source of great joy for us as parents."

"We wish them a lifetime of happiness and are very excited for their future together."

William and Catherine were delighted, although their public expression of congratulations was quietly understated, in keeping with royal protocol. Released through Kensington Palace, the Cambridges' tweet read: "We are very excited for Harry and Meghan. It has been wonderful getting to know Meghan and to see how happy she and Harry are together." Will and Kate no doubt privately shared their delight with Harry over finally finding The One.

After his formal felicitations were released, William joked that maybe this meant Harry would quit popping by Apartment 1A to raid his fridge and "stop scrounging my food, which he's done for the last few years!"

The Duke of Cambridge can rest easy in that regard. Meghan has undoubtedly stocked the Nott Cott kitchen with healthy food, and the couple love to cook at home, as evidenced by the most famous roast chicken dinner of the twenty-first century.

Speaking outside London's Foundling Museum where she had an engagement that day, Catherine said, "William and I are absolutely thrilled. It's such exciting news. It's a really happy time for any couple and we wish them all the best and hope they enjoy this happy moment."

A spokesman for Buckingham Palace on behalf of Their Majesties said, "The Queen and the Duke of Edinburgh are delighted for the couple and wish them every happiness."

Harry's proud father and Camilla, the Duchess of Cornwall,

tweeted: "We're thrilled. We're both thrilled. We hope they will be very happy indeed."

The following day, Camilla reiterated her happiness for the couple, telling a reporter, "Absolutely thrilled—it's brilliant. And as I said, America's loss is our gain. We're all absolutely delighted. Sometimes in a climate where we're surrounded by a lot of bad news, it's a real joy to have a bit of good news for once."

To a royal, everyone was wild about Meghan, delighted to welcome her into the family.

Well-wishes poured in from two governments as well.

Britain's Prime Minister Theresa May, undoubtedly pleased to be discussing something other than Brexit, issued a statement declaring: "I would like to offer my very warmest congratulations to HRH Prince Harry and Meghan Markle upon their engagement. This is a time of huge celebration and excitement for two people in love, and on behalf of myself, the Government, and the country, I wish them great happiness for the future."

Interrupting a speech at a Labour rally, Her Majesty's Leader of the Opposition Jeremy Corbyn also congratulated the newly affianced couple. "I wish them well. I hope they have a great time and great fun together and having met Harry a couple of times, I'm sure they will have great fun together!" Corbyn went on to praise the way both Harry and William have drawn attention to mental health conditions across the United Kingdom.

Harry's longtime friends former U.S. president Barack Obama and the former first lady tweeted a shout-out to the prince and his American sweetheart: "Michelle and I are delighted to congratulate Prince Harry and Meghan Markle on their engagement. We wish you a lifetime of joy and happiness together."

Meghan's *Suits* family quickly expressed their happiness for their costar as well. Her onscreen partner Patrick J. Adams joked on Twitter: "She said she was just going out to get some milk."

Wendell Pierce, who played Meghan's father, tweeted: "Congratulations to my TV daughter Meghan Markle and Prince Harry on the news of their wedding engagement. Harry you have her TV father's blessing. Robert Zane approves."

As the announcement was breaking online and on broadcast television across the globe, Harry and Meghan stepped outside for a photo op in Kensington Palace's Sunken Garden. Harry was wearing a blue suit, a white shirt, and a blue necktie, the same colors his mother wore when her engagement to his father was announced. Meghan was wrapped in a belted white trench coat from Line the Label, a Toronto brand founded in 2000 that is also a favorite with actresses Kate Bosworth and Sarah Jessica Parker. The company has since renamed that style The Meghan. Her bone suede high-heeled gillies were Aquazurra's Matilde style.

A few hours after the photo call, the couple returned to Nott Cott to grant an exclusive interview to the BBC's Mishal Husain. Harry was still wearing his blue suit. Meghan looked dressy but understated in a sleeveless Nile-green sheath dress by the Italian brand P.A.R.O.S.H.

Holding hands the entire time, as they nestled side by side on a white sofa, Meghan and Harry appeared thoroughly in love and at ease in front of the camera, even finishing each other's sentences. Meghan often answered a question for both of them, subtly glancing to Harry before she spoke to make sure he was cool with that. As a couple, they were completely in harmony. Unsurprisingly, given Meghan's profession, she seemed more comfortable with a live, on-camera interview. Harry has a tell when he's a bit anxious or nervous; he places his palm protectively over his midsection.

The spark between them was immediate, a beaming Meghan told Ms. Husain. She and Harry discussed their mutual enthusiasm for humanitarian issues at length on their first date. "One of the first things we connected on was how passionate we were about seeing change. That's how we got 'date two' in the books," she said.

According to Harry, it led to them "very quickly" saying, "Well, what are we going to do tomorrow? We should meet again." They both took out their "diaries" and searched for the next mutually available date in their calendars.

Meghan disagreed with Ms. Husain's categorization of their relationship—a year and a half prior to Harry's proposal—as a whirlwind. The public might not have learned about their romance until later on; but for the first several months, she and Harry had been able to keep their secret and were therefore able to allow things to develop at their own natural pace.

"Everything that I know *about* him I know *through* him, as opposed to growing up around whatever news stories or tabloids, or whatever else," Meghan told Ms. Husain, explaining that being American, she grew up knowing very little about the royal family. So she had no preconceived notions about Harry, just as he had none about her, having never seen her on television.

"Everything about him and his family was what he would share with me, and vice versa. So for both of us it was a really authentic and organic way to get to know each other," Meghan added.

For Harry, it was "hugely refreshing" to become involved with a woman who didn't think she already knew him and who also wasn't from his social circle.

Because theirs was a long-distance relationship and they had to juggle myriad commitments, including Meghan's punishing shooting schedule, they were nevertheless willing to put in the effort to make it work. Harry turned to Meghan. "I don't think you know what time zone you've been in for the last year and a half."

Meghan started to laugh. "No, no, I didn't!"

As for knowing what she was letting herself in for by marrying into Britain's royal family, Meghan admitted, "I think I can very safely say, as naive as it sounds now, having gone through this learning curve in the past year and a half, I did not have *any* understanding of just what it would be like." Looking to Harry for confirmation, she added, "I don't think either of us understood, even though we both knew it would be—"

"I tried to warn you as much as possible," Harry gently interjected. He shook his head. "But I think *both* of us were totally surprised by the reaction after the first five or six months we had to ourselves. . . . You can have as many conversations as you want and try to prepare as much as possible; but we were totally unprepared for what happened after that."

"The scrutiny," Ms. Husain prompted.

In addition to the negative press surrounding Meghan's ethnicity, nationality, and even her profession (as it pertains to her talent, as well as to her suitability to be a royal in the first place), there has been an assumption, to some degree, that the media attention that began after the royal relationship was made public, and which will accompany Meghan for the rest of her life, will be an easy transition for her because as an actress she's accustomed to photo shoots, red carpets, and promotional appearances.

But Meghan was quick to dispel any misconceptions that her career provided a solid preparation for the tsunami. "I've never been part of tabloid culture," she told the BBC. "I've never been in pop culture to that degree, and lived a relatively quiet life even though I focus so much on my job. So that was a really stark difference out of the gate."

Meghan made the determination early on not to read any of the comments, positive or negative, about their relationship; it was just healthier to use that energy to "focus on us."

"On us," Meghan repeated as Harry said the phrase in tandem. The couple smiled at each other, every inch an "us."

For those who had expected the prince to pop the question in grand fashion, perhaps during their romantic helicopter ride over the Zambezi River while he and Meghan were on holiday in Africa in August 2017, the modest proposal did come as a surprise. Although the media was deprived of such playful headlines as HARRY KNEELS; VICTORIA FALLS, the proposal, when it came—and later than pundits had predicted—was so normal. So *not* royal. The forgoing of the princely grand gesture for the spontaneous moment of simply adorable domesticity is more in keeping with the romance of couples such as Victoria and Albert.

"And it was just an amazing surprise. It was so sweet and natural and very romantic," Meghan said. She and Harry gazed lovingly into each other's eyes as if they were reliving the moment. Meghan added, "He got on one knee."

"Of course," Harry interjected.

"Was it an instant yes from you?" Ms. Husain asked Meghan.

"Yes!" she replied enthusiastically. Turning to Harry, Meghan added, "As a matter of fact, I could barely let you finish proposing." Still speaking to and looking at her fiancé, Meghan, replaying the moment, said, "Can I say yes now?"

Harry said, "She wouldn't let me finish [proposing]. She said 'Can I say yes? Can I say yes?' And then there was hugs, and I had the ring on my finger; and I said, 'Can I give you the ring?'" Harry grew more excited as he described the marriage proposal, play by play. "And she was like, 'Oh, yes, the ring!' So it was a really nice moment. It was just the two of us and I think I managed to catch her by surprise."

Harry designed the engagement ring himself, in partnership with Her Majesty's jeweler Cleave & Company. Touched by that gesture, Meghan said, admiring it, "It's beautiful—and it's incredible."

"And it should stay on your finger," Harry murmured, looking at it.

"Of course!" Meghan said, laughing.

The band is a simple circle of Welsh yellow gold—Meghan's favorite, Harry said proudly—with three diamonds. The center diamond came from Botswana, which has great sentimental significance to Harry. "The little diamonds on either side are from my mother's jewelry collection, to make sure that she's with us on this crazy journey together," he told Ms. Husain.

MEGHAN WAS DEEPLY moved as well as by the richly personal sentiment behind the design. "I think everything about Harry's thoughtfulness and his inclusion [of Diana's stones in the ring] and, obviously, not being able to meet his mom—it's so important to me to know that she's a part of this with us; and to be able to meet his aunts and . . . different people who were important to his mom, I'm able in some way to know a part of her through them, and of course through him." Meghan turned to Harry again. "And it's incredibly special to have this [ring], which links where *you* come from; and Botswana, which is important to us and—it's perfect." Meghan smiled.

"What do you think your mother would have thought of Meghan?" Ms. Husain asked the prince.

Harry grew wistful. Meghan appeared to clasp his hand more tightly. Fixing her gaze on *him*, her eyes brimmed with compassion, as if she were letting Harry know that it was okay for him to take his time, to be candid, open, emotional. She was right there for him and always would be. "They would have been thick as thieves, without question," Harry said of Meghan and his mum. "I think she would be over the moon, jumping up and down and so excited for me. But then I also believe that she would have been best friends with Meghan. It is days like today when I really miss having her around."

Meghan appeared to be holding back tears. She swallowed hard.

"I miss being able to share the happy news," Harry continued. "But I'm sure she's—"

"She's with us," Meghan said softly, knowing just when to jump in.

"She's with us," Harry echoed. "You know—jumping up and down somewhere else."

Harry admitted that he felt "responsible for" Meghan, "from Day One, or at least from a couple of months in," for what her life would be like as a royal. Moreover, he realized that he and Meghan needed to have some "frank conversations" if their relationship was going to go the distance.

"When I suddenly realized I know that I'm in love with this girl and I hope she loves me," he had to tell Meghan, "Look, what you're letting yourself in for is a big deal. It's not easy for anybody. But she chooses me and I choose her; and therefore, whatever we have to tackle together, or individually, will always be us as a team."

"It's so nicely said, isn't it?" Meghan said, beaming as she snuggled into Harry.

As they laughed, touched, at times even blushed, maintaining eye contact throughout, their interview was hardly the embarrassing "Whatever *love* is" debacle Harry's parents gave the press a generation earlier, where Diana was asked to stand on the stair below Charles so that she would not appear taller than he was; or even the relatively staid, albeit charming interview that William and Kate did in November 2010, which seemed groundbreaking at the time.

"She's capable of anything," Harry said proudly. "There's a hell of a lot that needs doing. Our relationship will always come first; but for us, we're both passionate about wanting to make change, especially for young people in the Commonwealth."

"Children?" asked Ms. Husain.

"Not currently, no," Harry deadpanned. Meghan laughed again. But they do plan to start a family eventually, he conceded.

Harry sees his own official role going forward as having three branches: first, to honor and extend his mother's legacy, particularly with regard to those affected with AIDS. He has inherited Diana's talent for communicating with all types of people from all over the world, especially children. Harry's work with Sentebale in Lesotho has already been effecting change there.

The second responsibility is to support the nonagenarian monarch, who has been steadily passing some of her duties to her grandchildren while allowing them to choose their own passion projects. And the third thread is his work, along with William and Kate, to remove the stigma surrounding mental health, especially in a culture where men and women are supposed to soldier on and not discuss their problems. The British government is supporting this initiative. They have the money, and the royals have the voice.

It seems likely that Meghan will add her voice to these projects as well.

She views her marriage to Harry not as leaving her past successes behind, but as an opportunity to generate different ones moving forward—a new chapter in her life. "Bear in mind," she told Ms. Husain, "I've been fortunate enough to work on a series for *seven years*; and to have that kind of longevity—once we hit the one-hundred-episode mark, I thought, Well, I've ticked that box—and I feel really proud of the work I've done there. And now it's time to"—smiling, she angled her body even more toward Harry and spoke directly, sweetly, and proudly to him—"as you said, work as a team. With you."

What Meghan has found "really exciting" as she transitions out of her acting career and into her role as a royal is that she can focus even more energy on the causes that are important to her. "Very early out of the gate you realize that once you have access or a voice that people are going to listen to, with that comes responsibility, which I take seriously. And in the same time, in these beginning few months . . . now, being boots on the ground in the UK, I'm excited to get to know more about the different communities here, smaller organizations, working on the same causes that I've always been passionate about, under this umbrella—and also to be able to go around the Commonwealth—"

"There's a lot to do," Harry agreed, finishing her sentence, as

Meghan nodded. "The fact that I fell in love with Meghan so quickly was confirmation to me that all the stars were aligned, that everything was just perfect. It was this beautiful woman who just literally tripped and fell into my life; I fell into her life; and the fact that I know she'll be unbelievably good at the *job* part of it as well is obviously a huge relief to me, because she'll be able to deal with everything else that comes with it. But we're a fantastic team, we know we are; and we hope to, over time, have as much impact on the things that we care about as much as possible."

Harry sees The Firm as a "team" as well. Perhaps he was trained to develop that optic in the army, or perhaps it was why he did well there. So when he was asked by Ms. Husain if Meghan would represent "something new" for the royal family, Harry deftly deflected the question.

If the interviewer was looking for the prince to discuss Meghan's race or nationality, or both, Harry wasn't biting. Instead, he replied that he viewed Meghan as another "member of the team" to carry out their engagements and their work, and to "try to encourage younger generations to see the world in the correct sense rather than perhaps having a distorted view." It's possible Harry meant *their* diversity is a microcosm of a more global sensibility, rather than representing the image of a passé colonial one; or he simply means that he and Meghan have a more hands-on approach to humanitarian work than previous generations of the royal family. Neither of them has ever been content just to cut ribbons. Both Meghan and Harry have become physically involved in their charities, building fences and wells, journeying to villages, and spending days helping to improve conditions. "We don't want to turn up, shake hands, but not get involved," Harry has said.

What Harry's comment may have meant is that he—along with William and Catherine—*is* keen to overhaul the British monarchy, to put a youthful modern face on the thousand-year-old institution. "The monarchy is a force for good, and we want to carry on the positive atmosphere that the Queen has achieved for over sixty years, but we won't be trying to fill her boots."

In 2017, *Hello!* magazine named Meghan their Woman of the Year. After her engagement was formally announced, she swiftly became one of the most famous and photographed women in the world. What's more, not only had Meghan won the heart of a prince, but she had so charmed the Queen of England that Her Majesty was breaking her own rules to allow Meghan to take part in all of the Sandringham Christmas events as if she were already one of the family.

On Wednesday, December 20, Meghan joined fifty members of the royal family for the Queen's annual pre-Christmas lunch at Buckingham Palace, arriving with Harry in a black Range Rover. A long-lensed photographer managed to snap a photo of her from the shoulders up. Although Meghan was seated and her ensemble was obscured by a shoulder harness, eagle-eyed fashionistas managed to identify her dress, which featured a mock turtleneck black-and-white guipure lace bodice and black crepe skirt, as the Nightshade Midi Dress from Self-Portrait, a London brand also popular with Kate. The frock sold out within hours after the image was posted online, likely by the time the royal family was enjoying a post-prandial brandy.

Her Majesty's pre-Christmas lunch marked Meghan's maiden opportunity to meet the Windsors who inhabit the family's outer orbit. Only the Queen's immediate family spends the holiday with her at Sandringham, so the luncheon is the sovereign's way of celebrating the season with the members of the extended clan.

Unfortunately, as welcoming as the royal corgis had been to Meghan, one member of the family felt it necessary to remind the American bride-to-be of her, well, roots.

Princess Michael of Kent, whose views on race are as progressive as Wallis Simpson's, if not George Wallace's, wore a large shiny blackamoor brooch pinned to her white jacket.

The blackamoors were African slave children who were brought to Britain's royal courts, primarily during the seventeenth and eighteenth centuries. They were costumed in exotic ensembles, with turbans, balloon trousers, and Turkish slippers, garments that constituted a romantic vision of the way the British imagined people dressed in Africa and the Ottoman empire. Treated as a charming curiosity, blackamoors served as page boys to members of the royal family. Having a blackamoor in one's train was a status symbol, akin at the time to owning a rare breed of lapdog.

Because Princess Michael was a woman who reportedly once told a group of black diners in a New York City restaurant to "Go back to the colonies!" few believed that she had just randomly pulled an old piece of jewelry out of the vault that morning. The personal history of the Czech-born "Princess Pushy" has been too well documented for her pin not to have been a deliberate slur, intended to "stick it" to the newest member of the family. In American culture, the blackamoor pin might be equated with a piece of costume jewelry resembling Aunt Jemima or a lawn jockey.

Photographs of Princess Michael wearing the offensive brooch went viral and she was vilified for her insensitivity, with calls for the Queen to ban her from future gatherings. The princess issued a toothless apology, claiming that the pin had been a gift from her husband Prince Michael and that she had worn it several times in the past without incident.

Sadly, the "colonial" attitude toward people of other races has been par for the course for decades among some of the senior royals. The nearly hundred-year-old gaffe-prone Duke of Edinburgh has put his foot in it numerous times on state visits, particularly when in Africa and Australia, where he has made ignorant and insensitive remarks to people of color. The Prince of Wales and

Camilla have also endeavored to suppress fits of uncomfortable giggles during tours abroad.

It has been, and will continue to be, up to the new generation of royals to move the British monarchy into the modern era.

The day after Meghan had to endure such a rude welcome from the Queen's officious cousin, her official engagement portraits with Harry were released. Fashion and celebrity photographer Alexi Lubomirski took the photographs at Frogmore, the private gardens situated within the Home Park, a private park adjoining Windsor Castle. Queen Victoria and her beloved consort Prince Albert, the most romantic couple in royal history, are buried together in the Royal Mausoleum at Frogmore.

Frogmore indeed derives its name from the multitude of frogs that dwell in this marshy area near the Thames. Any mention of frogs will lead to that of kissing and marrying princes, and the inevitable fairy-tale comparisons!

The engagement photos did allow Meghan to have a Cinderella moment after all. Some critics derided her choice to pose in a $75,000—and semi-sheer—ball gown with an embellished bodice designed by the British-based Australian house Ralph & Russo. After all, Harry seems to own just one blue suit that he trots out for all special occasions.

But how often does a biracial American girl from View Park–Windsor Hills marry a Windsor?

Who *wouldn't* wear a phenomenal gown in her formal engagement portraits with him?

The day was all about Meghan and Harry's personal lives, yes. But it was also a milestone for the British monarchy, for an American woman, and for that particular American. Aware of the importance and the impact of the occasion, Meghan recognized that it required a special dress. Yet whether she realized it or not, the Ralph & Russo gown Meghan wore for her engagement photos is also reminiscent of the one Halle Berry wore in 2002 when she became the first African American to win the Academy Award for Best Actress. Berry, like Meghan, is biracial: her mother is white. Ms. Berry's first words, after tears amid a standing ovation were "This moment is so much bigger than me."

There was additional messaging involved in Meghan's wardrobe choices. Both her gown and the sweater she wore in the black-and-white photographs were by British designers. She displayed the same sartorial acumen that Michelle Obama and the Duchess of Cambridge have for wearing native designers on their home turf. When Meghan was filming *Suits* in Toronto, she was known for advancing the work of Canadian labels.

The sweater was designed by Meghan's new friend Victoria Beckham, who in her previous persona as Posh Spice posed with the adolescent Harry at a Spice Girls concert in Pretoria.

For any photo shoot to be successful, the subjects and the photographer need to establish a rapport. One reason Harry and Meghan's engagement photos *are* so engaging, and the two of them appear so at ease in front of the camera, acting as if no one is watching them just be in love, is because they were at ease with the man behind the lens.

Alexi Lubomirski has much in common with both Meghan and Harry, from his mixed background to his childhood experiences to his passion for giving back to those who need it most. Born in England to a Peruvian English mother and a French Polish father, Alexi is a prince of the Polish Lubomirski dynasty. But after his parents separated when he was only eight years old, he moved to Botswana. Three years later, Lubomirski's stepfather gave him his first camera. Lubomirski is the author of *Princely Advice for a Happy Life*, an etiquette book he wrote for his two young sons on the virtue of behaving in a manner befitting a prince living in the twenty-first century. Proceeds from his book sales go to the charity Concern Worldwide, which helps the poorest people on the planet to break out of the cycles of poverty and hunger.

Of his royal assignment, Lubomirski said, "It was an incredible honor to be asked to document this wonderful event, but also a great privilege to be invited to share and be a witness to this young couple's love for one another. I cannot help but smile when I look at the photos that we took of them, such was their happiness together."

AS THE PAIR continues their journey toward the altar, Meghan has moved across the pond to London to be Harry's fiancée; and gave up, or is in the process of giving up, her lifestyle blog, her Instagram feed, her American citizenship, her religion, and her acting career. Before she became engaged to Harry, Meghan was shortlisted to be a Bond Girl in Daniel Craig's next 007 film. The producers' brief had been to find a rising star, preferably someone American or Canadian. Meghan had caught their eye as Rachel Zane. However, as her relationship with Harry heated up, she was removed from the running. The producers had a hunch she would soon become unavailable.

But, to paraphrase a line in Mel Brooks's *Young Frankenstein*, what did Harry give up for *her*?

In advance of their wedding, Harry has given Meghan quite possibly one of the best gifts of all. Meghan is a nonsmoker, and he has kicked the habit. Smoking is officially banned at Kensington Palace, and Nottingham Cottage is situated on its grounds, but when has Harry been known to obey the rules?

Harry has *always* either ignored the rule book or shredded it. He and Meghan already broke royal protocol by being openly affectionate during their first official royal engagement. They held hands and slipped their arms about each other's waists during a visit to Nottingham for a World AIDS Day celebration on December 1, 2017. The public was delighted to see Harry so happy and in love. They took to Meghan immediately, and the affection was mutual. Meghan and Harry were just as demonstrative in

January 2018, when they visited Reprezent Radio in Brixton to learn how young people in the community were using broadcast media for social impact.

However, certain things about the royal family are set in stone, and one of them is the Court Calendar, which is very much like a twenty-first-century version of a sixteenth-century Elizabethan royal progress. Various months of the year, as well as certain important holidays, are traditionally enjoyed at specific royal residences.

Christmases are always spent at Sandringham, the Queen's official residence in Norfolk. Built in 1870, this redbrick manor house has been the private home to four generations of British monarchs. Edward VII threw lavish parties there. Queen Elizabeth's father died there.

The Queen has an ironclad rule that only married couples may reside in the main house during the Christmas holiday. Although Meghan enjoyed her first Christmas with her future in-laws in high style, she would not be allowed to stay with Harry in the main house until after their wedding in May 2018. Therefore, rather than endure a Victorian-style separation, the couple bunked with William and Kate and their children in Anmer Hall, the Cambridges' ten-bedroom, eighteenth-century country home in Norfolk, approximately two miles east of Sandringham.

Nevertheless, Meghan is the first royal fiancée ever to be permitted to participate in the family's Christmas celebration and to attend church with them on Christmas morning. When the announcement was made that the Queen was breaking one of her own previously inviolable traditions to welcome Meghan sooner rather than later, some members of the press suddenly became dreadfully prudish. What in blazes had happened? they cried. Kate Middleton was engaged to Prince William by Christmas in 2010, and she received no such invitation!

But the explanation was simple. Catherine wished to spend her last Christmas as a "civilian" with her tight-knit family at their home in Berkshire; and in the intervening seven years, the Queen mellowed a bit. She and Prince Philip are now both in their nineties, and above all they wished to see Harry happy. If that meant including Meghan at Sandringham when she was still a royal fiancée, then time must march on.

During Harry's deployment in Afghanistan in December 2007, he insisted that "Christmas is overrated anyway." He never could have dreamt that exactly ten years later, his grandmother would give him such a magnanimous present by inviting his intended to join the family at Sandringham. In yet another break with tradition, it may be the first non-gag gift ever bestowed by one of the Windsors on another.

At the age of ninety-one, Elizabeth II, it seemed, was the one taking after Harry to become a royal rule breaker!

Sandringham sits on twenty thousand acres of parklands, gardens, orchards, farms, and woods. The estate grows and harvests its own Christmas trees, so every year there are invariably a number of gorgeously decorated stunners on display throughout the home.

Every Christmas, a Norfolk spruce is chopped down by staff members and decorated with ornaments that belonged to Queen Victoria. Fairy lights are already twinkling on the tree by the time the Queen arrives a few days later. She always has the honor of adding the tinsel and topping the tree with its star.

When Harry was a boy, he would arrive with his family on Christmas Eve, when he would receive his holiday card from "Granny and Gramps." The royal children always had their own Christmas cake.

On Christmas Eve, after their eight P.M. drinks, the family assembles for a black-tie dinner. The menu typically consists of Norfolk shrimp, and lamb or game that has been shot on the estate itself, washed down with champagne and vintage wines. After dinner, the royal family pops bespoke paper crackers that have been embellished with gold or silver crowns. Christmas crackers traditionally have little prizes inside; the Queen evidently loves to read the corny little jokes that pop out when the crackers explode.

In another tradition that dates back to Victoria and Albert, presents are exchanged on Christmas Eve rather than on Christmas morning. The family gathers in the White Drawing Room, a comfortable salon with a cream-colored sofa, white-on-white boiserie paneling, mirrored doors, and glass-fronted curio cabinets. The ceiling is painted in a trompe l'oeil effect with blue sky and birds winging overhead. Wall sconces, the crackling logs in the fireplace, and the sparkling lights on the tree provide the only illumination.

The royal family does not lavish expensive Christmas gifts on each other. Only gag gifts are exchanged. A separate trestle table covered with a white cloth and piled with presents is set up for each family member. As a boy, Harry was very easy to shop for because he loved anything to do with the army: toy soldiers, toy tanks, and miniature army uniforms.

Meghan's gift to the Queen, a singing toy hamster on a rope, was a great success. Thoroughly delighted, Her Majesty evidently burst out laughing, but had only a few moments to amuse herself with Meghan's present before the royal corgis made a grab for it.

On Christmas morning, the royals awaken to stockings filled with treats before attending the eleven A.M. service at St. Mary Magdalene, a church on the Sandringham estate that dates to the early sixteenth century. On December 25, 2017, as she walked with the rest of the royal family to church, Meghan was attired head to toe in shades of fawn, wearing a beige baby alpaca trench by the Canadian brand Sentaler, American Stuart Weitzman brown suede boots, a $1,550 two-toned Chloé Pixie bag, and a cinnamon-hued toque designed by milliner to the royals Philip Treacy. The hat sparked the most discussion, as it bore more than a passing resemblance to, variously, an acorn, a chocolate truffle; and to its detractors, the poo emoji. The role of royal fiancée on her way to worship with her new family in front of hundreds of fans and all manner of cameras was one that Meghan appeared understandably nervous to play at times; and she kept her arm tucked inside Harry's during most of the walk to church. It could have been the hat—the first time her ability to blend the traditional with a dash of Hollywood élan seemed to have deserted her.

The route to St. Mary Magdalene is customarily lined with visitors waiting to catch a glimpse of the royal family. It was especially crowded in 2017, as well-wishers hoped to see Meghan and Harry, as well as the Duchess of Cambridge, so they could offer their congratulations both to the newly engaged couple and the mum-to-be. Tourists began arriving as early as two A.M. on Christmas morning in order to secure an optimal vantage. One young American took the opportunity to propose to his girlfriend as they waited for the Windsors.

On their return from church, the royal family traditionally changes into formal attire for luncheon in the dining room at 1:15. They are served off china, crystal, and silver, with a menu in French that resembles an American Thanksgiving or Christmas dinner—roast turkey and all the fixings. The dining room, painted in a shade of pistachio known as Braemar green, with walnut and mahogany paneling, has a dark, intimate atmosphere, made all the more cozy with the addition of a pair of Christmas trees sparkling with fairy lights.

The $298 dress from the Canadian brand Club Monaco that Meghan wore during the Christmas lunch with her new family was the dark cherry polyester velvet midi-length Tay dress with fluttering cap sleeves. But what made it a rather daring choice for the afternoon (not to mention the future in-laws) and sent the Internet aflutter was the wrap dress's plunging neckline.

Every hour is accounted for. The royal family's Christmas Day tradition continues at three P.M., when they adjourn to the Saloon, a vast, high-ceilinged room decorated in shades of soft cream. Brussels tapestries adorn the walls. A trio of fluted Corinthian columns supports three Romanesque arches, above which is a balcony worked in wooden tracery. The entire unit is a hodgepodge of architectural elements that looks as if it had been imported from a church into a high Victorian manse.

The television in the Saloon is turned on so that everyone can watch the Queen's Christmas address. Afterward, it's usually a good time to walk off lunch, because tea is served promptly at five P.M.; and no one wants to miss the traditional Christmas sweets—brandy snaps, mince pies, and the Yule log.

In 2017, looking like a grandmotherly angel in snowy white, the Queen delivered her sixtieth annual Christmas broadcast. Seated at a desk topped with photos of herself and Prince Philip, and a double frame of her great-grandchildren Prince George and Princess Charlotte, the monarch opened with an excerpt from her very first televised message to her subjects in 1957, then added with a wry remark, "the presenter has evolved somewhat, as has the technology she described." Her first few annual addresses were given over the wireless, after her ascension in 1952. Her Majesty traditionally speaks of faith and family, peace on earth, and goodwill to all; but with grim times comes the recognition of tragedy as well.

In 2017, the Queen mentioned the victims of the Caribbean hurricanes and the two terrorist attacks on British soil, as well as those who perished in the Grenfell Tower high-rise fire. The Queen mentioned Meghan obliquely in the context of looking forward to welcoming new members into the family in 2018, a sentiment that would also apply to William and Catherine's third child, due to arrive in April.

There's no telly watching permitted in the Saloon during the evening. That's when the board games come out—except for

Monopoly, which the royal family is forbidden from playing—because, as Prince Andrew explained, "it gets too vicious." They can always step away from the dice and play charades, which remains a popular improv game with the Windsors. Harry evidently takes after his grandmother: the Queen is said to be an excellent mimic, and both are terrific charades players. With her acting skills, Meghan would probably excel at charades as well.

The annual Boxing Day shoot on December 26 is a big deal, especially to the Windsor men. Various birds of a feather meet their demise, including pheasant, partridge, quail, duck, and woodcock. Hunters eat lunch in a hut on the grounds, dining on venison stew, mashed potatoes, and sausages with fried plum pudding; and drinking whisky and tea to keep warm. When Harry was a boy, he couldn't wait to be old enough to join his older relatives. His mother hated such excursions ("they're always shooting things"). Meghan, who is very comfortable in her own skin, felt no pressure to "shoot things" just because the Windsors enjoy it so much, and out of respect for his fiancée's compassion for animals and her dislike of blood sports, Harry did not participate in the 2017 Boxing Day shoot. Somewhere, Diana is smiling.

The couple capped off their holiday by spending New Year's Eve in Monaco. Harry and Meghan flew coach to the South of France and took a quick helicopter ride to the tiny principality, where they met up with a group of friends for a glamorous celebration.

After Harry told BBC's Radio 4 that Meghan had an "amazing Christmas" with his relatives, adding, "I suppose it's the family she's never had," Meghan's half sister Samantha, who currently resides in Florida, lashed out at her future in-law and at the media, tweeting, "Actually she has a very large family who were always there with her and for her. Our household was very normal, and when Dad and Doria divorced, we made it like it was so she had two houses. No one was estranged, she was just too busy." What followed was a plug for Samantha's book. Samantha's brother and Meghan's father also took umbrage at Harry's remark.

There is nothing in Samantha's tweet that would seem to contradict anything Meghan has ever said about growing up Markle. But what Harry had, perhaps awkwardly, been trying to express, was that some of Meghan's family had not always been there for her *lately*.

Namely Samantha. After Meghan's romance with Harry was made public, her older sister was coaxed out of the woodwork to dish the dirt and had terribly *naughty* things to say about Meghan. It makes one wonder if, as Samantha has claimed, she wishes her sister well and her tell-all is filled with only *nice* things about her, why then does she use a nasty nickname to refer to Meghan in the book's title?

Family baggage aside, Meghan required a sizable suitcase for her first Christmas with the Windsors. They adore dressing up for the holidays, and multiple changes of clothing were a requirement. In many ways, it's still one long Edwardian house party. Five changes of ensemble were mandated for Christmas Day alone. A peek inside Meghan's trunk would have revealed evening gowns, day dresses, smart suits, and casual clothes, in case she changed her mind about the Boxing Day shoot—or just wanted to take a long walk with Harry through Sandringham's vast acreage.

Except for the hats, the Barbour jackets (she does own several), and the Wellies, she might as well have been packing for a *Suits* promotional tour.

## American Princess

Keen to have a more intimate wedding—by royal standards—Harry and Meghan also didn't want to draw comparisons either to the 2011 nuptials of William and Catherine, which took place in Westminster Abbey, or the marriage of Harry's parents, which was the first royal wedding to be held in London's spectacular (and cavernous) St. Paul's Cathedral.

For their ceremony, Harry, the first British royal to wed an American on his home turf, chose a venue that has sentimental meaning to them both. On Saturday, May 19, 2018, they will tie the knot in St. George's Chapel at Windsor Castle. The wedding reception will be held inside the castle in the vast red-carpeted St. George's Hall, a hallmark of medieval heraldry. The cream-colored walls are adorned with portraits, alternating with armored knights standing atop pedestals represented by St. George's shield. Standing on the floor below them are a series of carved busts resting on tall columns.

Dating back more than a thousand years to 1066, the thousand-room Windsor Castle has the most storied history of all of Great Britain's royal residences, a constant through every reign. Harry visited the castle frequently when he was growing up, especially when he was a student at Eton, just a stone's throw across the Thames.

The royal family itself has a deeply personal connection to St. George's Chapel. The chapel itself, which dates to 1528, is the traditional site of funerals and memorial services. Several famous royals, including ten kings, among them Henry VIII, are interred there. It's also the site of many family christenings—including Prince Harry's—as well as weddings between royal couples who prefer to exchange their vows in a more intimate venue. Harry's first cousin Princess Eugenie will marry her fiancé, Jack Brooksbank, in the chapel a few months after Meghan and Harry walk down the aisle.

Sitting atop the facade of St. George's Chapel are seventy-six heraldic statues representing fourteen different animals, the Queen's Beasts. The original sculptures dated to the sixteenth century. However, Christopher Wren, the architect of St. Paul's Cathedral in London, thought they spoiled the chapel's aesthetics, so he ordered them removed. The current Beasts were placed there in 1925 after a renovation; they represent emblems of Great Britain and long-dead royals—among them the lion of England, the red dragon of Wales, the unicorn of Edward III, and the panther of the Seymour family, included because Jane Seymour is buried at St. George's Chapel beside her husband Henry VIII.

The chapel's fifteenth-century fan vaulted quire, where Meghan's and Harry's closest relations will likely be seated during the wedding ceremony, is hung with the colorful heraldic banners of the members of the Order of the Garter, and each stall is surmounted by their respective crests. The large stained-glass window above the altar, which has been restored many times and now features the images of seventy-five kings, princes, saints, and popes, refracts light like thousands of precious gemstones onto the black-and-white-tiled floor. Gaze skyward and you will see Tudor red and white roses concealing the seams in the vaulting. Worshipers are watched over by a continuous frieze of two hundred and fifty carved angels.

Compared to Westminster Abbey or St. Paul's Cathedral, St. George's Chapel conveys a more "human" and intimate scale, as it can seat only about 800 people. The most recent royal marriage performed there was the May 17, 2008, union of Princess Anne's son Peter Phillips to Canadian Autumn Kelly. Before embarking on a professional career as a management consultant, Autumn had worked as a bartender, model, and—gasp—actress. Prince Charles celebrated his marriage to Camilla Parker Bowles in St. George's Chapel, although they did not have a church wedding there. Instead, having taken their vows in a civil ceremony in Windsor Guildhall earlier in the day, they received a blessing for their marriage inside the chapel.

St. George's Chapel is also the spiritual home to the Order of the Garter, the world's oldest order of chivalry. Inspired by Arthurian legend, the order was created by Edward III in 1348; its motto, *honi soit qui mal y pense*, translates to "Evil to him who thinks evil."

Among those who might pause to consider these words are Princesses Eugenie and Beatrice, the daughters of the divorced Duke and Duchess of York, Prince Andrew and Sarah Ferguson. They were reportedly not fond of Kate Middleton because of her middle-class origins; and Catherine's beauty, poise, and popularity continues to eclipse theirs. Now they are said to be envious of the Queen's swift acceptance of Meghan into the family. The princesses are evidently mortified that a woman of Meghan's background would marry Harry (demonstrating that *common* is a word that applies equally to one's behavior). Apparently, the two younger Yorks remain chagrined that Harry broke up with their aristocratic friend Cressy Bonas—to *them* a more suitable royal bride—although there were myriad reasons that Harry and Cressy were a mismatch in the long run.

According to several sources, including *Woman's Day*, the princesses have seethed for some time over the Queen's easy acceptance of an American commoner into the bosom of the royal family, as well as a perception fostered by their father Prince Andrew that Her Majesty favors Prince Charles's family over theirs. For a pair of young women who wore hats to William and Catherine's wedding that directly echoed those worn by the beastly stepsisters in the Disney classic *Cinderella*, Beatrice and Eugenie might wish to emulate kinder role models when they consider their headgear for Harry's wedding to Meghan.

HARRY'S REPUTATION AS a rebel remained intact, even when it came to his wedding plans. He broke a royal tradition by choosing to get married on a weekend. The announcement of the wedding date had both traditionalists and sports fans in a tizzy. May 19 is the same day that Anne Boleyn, Henry VIII's second wife, was executed in 1536 after a sham trial on the grounds of high treason and infidelity. (But perhaps new love erases bad karma?) Yet—horrors—after football (soccer to Americans) fans realized that the FA Cup final was scheduled to be played on May 19, 2018, they became miffed at the prospect of having to choose which event to watch—or attend. Prince William, who is the president of the Football Association, usually attends the final and presents the trophy to the winning club.

Kensington Palace assured football fans that the timing of the events would not clash. The celebration of Harry and Meghan's nuptials would begin at noon, and the footie match would kick off several hours later, at five-thirty. The most affected party would be Prince William, who would have to dash the twenty-three miles back and forth between the two, in his effort to be present at all ceremonies and receptions, making it one of the busiest days of his life that hasn't involved the birth of one of his children.

Another break with royal tradition that Harry and Meghan made was the choice to get married in the month of May. Queen Victoria refused to permit any of her large brood to wed during the month, observing a popular superstition of the day "Marry in May; rue the day." And ever since, nearly every royal couple—even those who have exchanged their vows in the spring, such as Prince William and Catherine Middleton, and Prince Charles and Camilla—have chosen a different month, opting for April instead. The only recent exception is the May 17, 2008, wedding of Peter Phillips and Autumn Kelly.

Although royal engagements tend to be quite short, allowing only a few months in which to plan and produce an event with such pomp, splendor, and pageantry, May 2018 was the soonest that Meghan and Harry could tie the knot. When it came time for the couple to select their wedding date, they had to be mindful of state events on the Court Calendar, as well as personal family ones.

The due date for the Duchess of Cambridge's third child was projected for April 2018. All thought it courteous to permit Catherine a few weeks of rest after the birth. On May 2, the family would be celebrating Princess Charlotte's third birthday.

Additionally, Harry's "gramps," the Duke of Edinburgh, who only recently retired from his royal duties, would celebrate his ninety-seventh birthday on June 10, 2018. Naturally, the prince was keen for his grandfather to share his wedding day.

One thing Queen Victoria might have been pleased by, however, was the news that Meghan might carry a sprig of myrtle in her wedding bouquet.

The romance surrounding these creamy white blooms dates back to the ancient Greeks and Romans, when myrtle was associated with Aphrodite and Venus, their respective goddesses of love and beauty, laughter, protection, and joy. Myrtle was also the symbol of marriage to the ancient Hebrews. As the centuries progressed, myrtle continued to be emblematic of love and desire, associated with sex because it was an ingredient in many love potions, believed to be helpful in creating and preserving love.

In English folklore it was held that "marriage will follow shortly after the myrtle blooms," so in Victorian times it became a symbol of fidelity. Queen Victoria herself was knowledgeable about the language of flowers. Prince Albert's grandmother gave her a cutting of myrtle, which was planted at Osborne House, the queen's residence on the Isle of Wight. When Victoria and Albert's oldest child, Princess Victoria, married Frederick III of Prussia, the future Kaiser Wilhelm I, in 1858, she carried a sprig from her mother's myrtle bush in her wedding bouquet, and a tradition was inaugurated. Myrtle has been a feature of royal wedding bouquets ever since.

Catherine Middleton's myrtle came from Victoria's own garden in Osborne. Meghan may continue this tradition in its classic form or opt to give it a more modern twist, incorporating the blue-black or amber myrtle fruit itself into her bouquet. Myrtle berry leaves are a glossy green with a spicy orange citrus scent. Another floral tradition would be to incorporate May's birth flower, the lily of the valley, whose light scent is said to lure the nightingale to his mate, and which Harry's mother carried in her bouquet when she married his father. It would be a sentimental nod to Diana; and in the language of flowers, the lily of the valley symbolizes both trust and the return of happiness: doubly apt metaphors for a May bride, like Meghan, who is marrying for the second time.

Because wedding bouquets tend to blend tradition with the bride's personal taste, it's possible that Meghan would include peonies in her bouquet. Years ago, on her Instagram page she posted photos of these large and lush but delicate blooms and declared her affinity for them. And shortly after she and Harry began dating, he sent her a lavish bouquet of the pink and white blossoms. Meghan posted a photo of the arrangement to her Instagram feed with the caption "Swooning over these. #London #peonies #spoiledrotten."

Meghan might also carry orange blossoms, which in times past were woven into a wreath and worn by royal brides as a head-dress with their veils, another tradition that began with Queen Victoria.

At many British weddings, including recent royal ones, young children act as bridesmaids and page boys rather than adult bridesmaids and groomsmen supporting the bridal couple. Harry has already invited his nephew and niece Prince George and Princess Charlotte to have some part in the ceremony. Little Ivy Mulroney, the daughter of Meghan's best friend and stylist Jessica Mulroney, is also expected to be in the wedding party. Jessica, who is a daughter-in-law of Canada's former prime minister Brian Mulroney, has also acted as a fashion stylist to the Duchess of Cambridge and Sophie Grégoire Trudeau, spouse of the current prime minister of Canada.

Yet the British tradition of children attending the bride, dressed like idyllic illustrations from a Victorian picture book, is not set in stone. In 1947, when Princess Elizabeth (now queen) married Prince Philip, and when her mother, Elizabeth Bowes-Lyon, married the Duke of York in 1923, adult bridesmaids—young ladies of aristocratic breeding and impeccable character—carried their long trains. The same was true of Queen Victoria's wedding in 1840.

It remains to be seen whether Meghan, being American, asks a number of her adult girlfriends to be her bridesmaids, as a way of honoring women who have been a special part of her life, as well as incorporating part of her own background and culture into the ceremony. She might even bend tradition by having her mother, her closest family member and lifelong best friend, be the parent to walk her down the aisle.

Harry, who was William's supporter (best man, to Americans) when he married Catherine Middleton in 2011, had not officially asked his big brother to return the honor as of early January 2018, although it's hard to imagine anyone else standing beside him. And Meghan may select a maid or a matron of honor. Just as Catherine Middleton broke with tradition when she asked her sister Pippa to be her maid of honor, Meghan may select one of her best friends to support her, rather than following the British tradition of selecting a chief bridesmaid. Meghan may also break another royal tradition and give a speech at her own wedding. If the publicity-shy Thomas Markle does attend, several sources reported that he may prefer not to stand up in front of eight hundred people to deliver a traditional father-of-the-bride toast, so Meghan will be the one to thank everyone on behalf of her family.

One person who is not likely to receive a wedding invitation is Meghan's ex-husband Trevor Engelson. After rebounding from his divorce with blond *Baywatch* starlet Charlotte McKinney, as of late 2017 Trevor was said to be dating Tracey Kurland, an attractive, also blond Los Angeles–based nutrition expert who reportedly interned at Twelfth Street by Cynthia Vincent, a clothing line popular with Pippa Middleton.

Trevor now works as a talent manager for actors, directors, screenwriters, and novelists. He's also the producer of *Heathers*, a TV version of the 1988 black comedy that starred Winona Ryder and Christian Slater, and the television series *Snowfall*, which focuses on the crack epidemic in 1980s Los Angeles.

In late 2017, Trevor shopped a script about a divorced couple who has to share custody of their child. But there's a twist! According to *Town & Country*, Trevor's official pitch reads: *Divorce is hard. Sharing custody is harder. Sharing custody with the British royal family when your wife marries a prince, in the unforgiving spotlight of London's tabloid media, is next level.*

It's fiction, of course. Trevor and Meghan had no children.

Another ex whose wedding invitation may get lost in the mail is Toronto chicken chef Cory Vitiello. He cheekily posted a mouthwatering video of rotisserie chickens roasting on a spit after Harry's self-deprecating revelation that they were "trying to roast" one in Nott Cott when he proposed to Meghan.

Cory may get all the "chicks," but in the end, Harry was the one who got the girl.

Like most modern couples, including William and Kate, Meghan and Harry are already taking an active role in their own wedding plans. A palace insider said that "Miss Markle has described it as reflecting a fairy-tale wedding, which of course is really what it is. Staff have been struck by how unbelievably happy they are together. They are having huge fun planning this. No one has ever seen Prince Harry quite like it." Rather than the usual process of delegating the wedding plans to the Lord Chamberlain's office in conjunction with the Master of the Household's Department, Harry has encouraged Meghan to be hands-on, as she has "great style and taste" and "a very clear idea of what she wants"—which sources have revealed may be a white and classic theme. According to Harry's communications secretary Jason Knauf, an American former public relations guru, Harry and Meghan's royal wedding will be "fun" and reflective of their relationship. "The couple of course want the day to be a special, celebratory moment for their friends and family. They also want the day to be shaped so as to allow members of the public to feel part of the celebrations too. This wedding, like all weddings, will be a moment of fun and joy that will reflect the characters of the bride and groom." At least one giant viewing screen will be erected in Windsor so the crowds can watch the ceremony live. In the absence of a palace balcony, the much-awaited first kiss is expected to take place on the steps of the chapel after the couple emerges as husband and wife. At one P.M., the newlyweds will take an open carriage ride through the streets of Windsor.

The fullest expression of the bride's character is always her choice of wedding gown. To that end, it was reported on December 20, 2017, that Kensington Palace had requested sketches from Tel Aviv–based wedding dress designer Inbal Dror. Her figure-hugging lavish designs, worn by A-listers such as Beyoncé and Naomi Watts, are more Hollywood princess than English princess—fashion-forward and hardly demure. The gowns' lavish detailing, with layers of lace and tulle as well as lengthy trains, could make them perfect for a royal wedding; but they are often sheer, with deeply plunging necklines—more red carpet and runway-ready than apt for most naves and apses.

The buttoned-up spectators from the Coworth Park Polo Club would truly faint into their Pimm's Cups at the sight of *that actress* in such a state of *negligee* walking down the aisle of St. George's Chapel to wed the sixth in line to the throne of England.

Because St. George's Chapel is a royal peculiar, meaning the monarch has direct jurisdiction over it, there are stricter and more conservative rules for bridal gowns than there would be if the royal marriage were taking place in a church or cathedral administered by a Church of England diocese. Even the wedding ceremony in St. George's Chapel will employ traditional, even arcane vocabulary, such as *wilt* and *thine*.

Any wedding dress designer would need to conform his or her usual aesthetic to the sartorial parameters of the chapel dress code. Ms. Dror understands the specific requirements of a royal wedding, however, and submitted a trio of long-sleeved preliminary sketches for approval, in several silhouettes from ball gown to mermaid to trumpet-skirted, featuring long sleeves, ruffles, and high lace collars, while retaining the embellishments for which her gowns have become famous. However, the very fact that preliminary sketches for prospective wedding gowns were leaked prompted skepticism that Ms. Dror had indeed been selected. When it comes to royal weddings, the identity of the bridal gown's designer tends to be shrouded in secrecy until the last moment; and in the past, British couturiers have been the chosen ones—because the brides have been British.

But Meghan and Harry are already breaking so many traditions that it's just as likely as it is not that Ms. Dror or another international couturier will be designing Meghan's wedding gown. And because Meghan isn't British, she may not have been instructed to or be expected to follow the unwritten mandate to select a UK designer. That said, when the news broke at the end of January 2018 that Meghan had chosen her bridal gown designer and was already in preliminary fittings, even though the identity of the couturier remained shrouded in secrecy, British designer Stewart Parvin, who is also the Queen's official dressmaker, was touted as the odds-on favorite.

What *is* likely is that Meghan's gown will be ivory or cream, which is a more flattering shade than pure white and which photographs better as well. The gown is also expected to have a long train, in keeping both with the occasion and the proportions of St. George's Chapel; but it's highly doubtful that Meghan's train would come anywhere near the record-breaking twenty-five-foot length of the train on Diana's gown, the longest in royal wedding history.

Meghan is also expected to wear British jewels for the wedding ceremony, including a tiara loaned to her by the Queen. Her wedding ring and Harry's are likely to be fashioned from a nugget of Welsh gold belonging to the monarch. Chips from the same nugget of gold from the Clogau mine in North Wales were used to fashion every royal wedding ring beginning with that of Harry's great-grandmum, the beloved late Queen Mother. That specific nugget has pretty much been exhausted, but Her Majesty gave Welsh gold to William for Catherine's wedding ring (he doesn't wear one); and it is expected she will do the same for Harry.

Meghan may also incorporate the Anglo-American wedding tradition of "something old, something new, something borrowed, something blue." The British used to add one more lucky element—"and a sixpence in her shoe." The "something blue" for

Americans is most often an elastic leg garter or a ribbon sewn into a hidden place inside the gown.

A great deal of excitement has also swirled around the couple's possible choice of wedding cake. People went nuts when word leaked that Meghan and Harry might choose a banana cake instead of the alcohol-soaked fruitcake that forms the customary top tier for British wedding cakes. The reason for the fruitcake, which everyone knows lasts forever, is so that it can indeed keep long enough to be served when the couple's first child is born. Speaking of inedible, a royal wedding cake typically takes three to four months to create, with or without a fruitcake. For a May date, the bakers had to begin their work in January. They start decorating it the week before the wedding day.

But Harry and Meghan may be going bananas, literally. And there may be some credence to the rumors. On October 31, 2017, after the royal romance had already been confirmed, Meghan posted a photo to her Instagram feed of two bananas with sleepy eyes, and smiles, and arms drawn on with a black Sharpie, cuddling—spooning—as it were, as the larger banana protectively embraces the smaller one. She captioned the photo: "Sleep tight xx."

Couples love to share a sweetly personal inside joke with their nearest and dearest on their special day. But a former royal chef, Darren McGrady, confirms that Prince Harry has always enjoyed banana desserts. A banana-caramel cake that he baked for Harry and William when they were growing up was a particular favorite.

Prince William went nontraditional for his groom cake, opting for one made of chocolate cookies. But to abandon the traditional fruitcake topper on the main cake would demonstrate, even in such a seemingly innocuous way, that Harry and Meghan, as a modern royal couple, may be opening a number of windows and daring to "let daylight in upon magic." Dispelling that sacrosanct aura of mystery surrounding the British royal family would send the Victorian critic Walter Bagehot, who coined the phrase, spinning in his grave.

The recipe for McGrady's banana-caramel cake, which he shared with ET online, can be found on the Internet.

Whether or not there was any truth to the rumor, as soon as Dole, America's most famous purveyor of the fruit, read the news that Harry and Meghan might be going bananas, they offered to make the couple's wedding cake.

ALTHOUGH MEGHAN HAS been married before, that will not pose any obstacle to a church wedding.

In the sixteenth century, Henry VIII famously broke with the Church of Rome in order to be able to divorce his first wife Catherine of Aragon and marry his inamorata Anne Boleyn in the hope of begetting a son. This led to the Reformation and the founding of the (Protestant) Church of England. In 1534, an act was passed declaring Henry, and all subsequent monarchs, to be the supreme head of the church. In Henry's day, and in the years before the British monarchy became a constitutional one, it was the sovereign's way or the highway. In other words, if Henry wanted a divorce, he got one. But as time went on, the Anglican Church came around to sharing the same view as Rome, refusing to recognize divorcés as having legally ended their marriages.

However, in the early twenty-first century, the Church of England clarified its position on divorce and now permits divorced people to remarry "in exceptional circumstances," although they must be asked a series of questions designed to ensure that "past hurts" have been healed and mistakes learned from. Since 2002, it has been up to the discretion of individual clergy as to whether they wish to officiate at a wedding where one or both persons have been divorced. A statement posted on the Church of England's website in February 2005, two months before Charles and Camilla wed, states that the blessings of the church are not denied to someone who remarries after divorce if the parish priest is willing to officiate.

The Archbishop of Canterbury is the senior bishop and principal leader of the Church of England, and Justin Welby, the current archbishop, said he was "absolutely delighted to hear the news that Prince Harry and Meghan Markle are engaged," stating, "I have met Prince Harry on a number of occasions and have always been struck by his commitment and passion for his charities, and his immense love for his family." On Twitter, he posted, "I wish them many years of love, happiness, and fulfillment—and ask that God blesses them throughout their married life together."

For over three hundred years, as a result of the Protestantism founded under Henry VIII and the Reformation in the sixteenth century, which led to centuries of religious tensions and violence sparked by the reigns of Catholic sovereigns Mary I and James II, Catholics were barred by a statute passed in 1701 known as the Act of Settlement from ascending the British throne, nor could members of the royal family in line for the throne marry someone of the Catholic faith.

As a recent example, to adhere both to state and church doctrine, Catholic Canadian Autumn Kelly converted to the Church of England so that her husband, Peter Phillips, who at the time was eleventh in line for the throne, did not have to forfeit his place in the succession.

Meghan was educated at a Catholic high school, but she is not a practicing Roman Catholic, nor was she raised as a Catholic. However, Kensington Palace has announced that Meghan will be baptized into the Church of England in advance of the wedding day. Moreover, per the Succession to the Crown Act 2013, persons who marry Roman Catholics are no longer disqualified from the line of succession.

It's traditional for the monarch to bestow a title upon royal newlyweds on their wedding day, and there has been speculation as to which title Harry will receive from his granny. Her Majesty granted a passel of titles to Prince William, the loftiest being the dukedom of Cambridge. Catherine Middleton became the Duchess of Cambridge, Countess of Strathearn, and Lady Carrickfergus, as well as Princess William of Wales on her wedding day.

The Queen might name Harry either Duke of Clarence or Duke of Sussex. Each title is an old one and carries its own historical baggage.

However, a troika of misbehaving Clarences may kibosh that royal appointment.

During the reign of Edward IV, the Duke of Clarence was his next younger brother George, who presented a threat to his throne. The fifteenth-century Duke of Clarence was handsome and devilishly charming; but his personality was a fatal combination of ambition, greed, envy, and dim-wittedness; and he had a dangerous case of wanting everything any of his brothers had—including titles, estates, offices, and the crown. Clarence was a serial traitor who conspired a whopping four times to topple Edward IV from the throne and claim the crown for himself. Long before the Duke of Gloucester (the future Richard III) usurped the throne, Clarence plotted to usurp it from their brother Edward. In an effort to keep Richard from his intended bride Anne Neville, Clarence kidnapped her. Contrary to Shakespeare's plot in *Richard III*, Richard truly loved Anne; they were childhood sweethearts.

In 1477, after Clarence ordered his followers to take up arms against their sovereign and be ready to "levy war against the king," Edward IV had Clarence arrested and charged with high treason. That year, Clarence spent his Christmas in the Tower of London.

Their brother Richard, in his office as high steward, speaking on behalf of Parliament, pronounced the death sentence against him on February 7, 1478. And on February 18, the twenty-eight-year-old Duke of Clarence was liquidated—literally. It's one of

Shakespeare's most memorable scenes, and the Bard evidently got that part right. Most scholars believe that Clarence was in fact drowned in a vat of Malmsey wine, his favorite potent potable—perhaps a perverse last request. After his death, his daughter Margaret (later Margaret Pole, 8th Countess of Salisbury) always wore a wine cock (the faucet or spigot from a wine cask) around her wrist. This unusual bracelet was accepted by her contemporaries as a tribute to her father, giving credence to the supposition about the duke's mode of execution.

The Hanoverian Duke of Clarence during the last quarter of the eighteenth century and through the Regency of the early nineteenth century was of course the future William IV, known for his two-decade domestic partnership with the comedic actress Dora Jordan. Ten children together and he dumped her.

And during Queen Victoria's lengthy reign, the second Hanoverian Duke of Clarence was her grandson Prince Albert Victor, known as Eddy. Eddy's apparent lack of academic and intellectual acumen made him the butt of rampant fear about such a dullard ever becoming king after his father Bertie, the Prince of Wales, had his turn. But worse than the prospect of a dope on the throne was that Eddy might not be eligible to reign at all. Whispers of "gross indecency"—the love that dare not speak its name—swirled around the young prince. Homosexuality was a felonious offense at the time, on the short list of items that could bar a man from inheriting the crown.

The homely Eddy, who also had his share of ill-advised female conquests, was accused of frequenting a notorious male brothel in London's Cleveland Street. When it was raided in 1889, Eddy was not there (nor was anyone else); but many were convinced at the time that he had gay predilections and that some of his own connections, including one of his equerries, were Cleveland Street customers who were covering for him.

Eddy eventually fell madly in love with a Catholic, Princess Hélène of Orléans, but she would not give up her faith to marry him.

Engaged to the impoverished but Anglican Princess Mary of Teck instead, twenty-eight-year-old Eddy died of influenza on December 14, 1892, thirty-one years to the day that his grandfather Prince Albert passed away. Consoled in her grief by Eddy's younger brother George, Mary ended up wedding him instead, becoming Queen Mary of England in 1910 when her husband, Prince Harry's great-great-grandfather, became George V.

Eddy's name was also put forward as the actual identity of Jack the Ripper, the serial murderer of a number of prostitutes in the autumn of 1888. While a pair of twentieth-century charlatans who sought to reopen the case by pinning the grisly attacks on the young Duke of Clarence were widely discredited, Eddy's name still comes up in Ripperology lore. Given the reputations of these three previous Dukes of Clarence, none of them paragons, it's unlikely that the Queen, who has a keen sense of history, will bestow this title on Harry.

The only previous Duke of Sussex was Prince Augustus Frederick, the sixth son of George III and Queen Charlotte, who was born on January 27, 1773. The title was conferred upon him on November 27, 1801. But Augustus's nuptial history is hardly illustrious. He wed twice, both times in contravention of his father's Royal Marriages Act 1772, which requires the monarch's consent to a marriage.

While he was touring Italy, Augustus met Lady Augusta Murray, the flaxen-haired second daughter of the 4th Earl of Dunmore. The pair had a secret wedding in Rome on April 4, 1793, when the prince was only twenty years old. Gus and Gussie were hauled back to London, where they had a second ceremony at St. George's Hanover Square, Westminster. Both marriages were performed without the knowledge or consent of Augustus's father the king. The marriage was annulled the following year, but the couple continued to live together—with their children—until 1801.

Thirty years later, Augustus once again flouted the law. By then he was a widower, Augusta having died the previous year. In 1831, the Duke of Sussex married Lady Cecilia Letitia Buggin, a pretty honey-blond widow who was the eldest daughter of the 2nd Earl of Arran. By then Augustus was Duke of Sussex, but his older brother George IV adamantly refused to accord Augustus's wife the title of Duchess of Sussex, despite his own extremely checkered marital history. George IV was an alleged bigamist, having secretly wed the Catholic Maria Fitzherbert ten years before he was compelled to marry his German first cousin Caroline of Brunswick—bribed by his father, who agreed to pay off his exorbitant debts if he did so.

It was Queen Victoria who gave Lady Cecilia a title in her own right. By then she had ditched her late husband's surname Buggin and taken her mother's name of Underwood. In 1840, Victoria created Lady Cecilia Duchess of Inverness so that she could accompany her husband to royal functions as an equal in rank. Because Cecilia had never been made Duchess of Sussex, for the first nine years of her marriage royal protocol had denied her the proverbial seat at the table.

The dukedom of Buckingham is also available; but a fair number of previous holders of the title conjure unpleasant memories as well. Edward Stafford, the 3rd Duke of Buckingham, was beheaded for treason by Richard III in 1521; although it could be argued that in contravening some of Richard's autocratic orders, he was acting in good conscience.

After Stafford's death the title became extinct; but it was revived in 1623 by James I, who bestowed it on his bisexual lover George Villiers, starting the clock again by naming Villiers the 1st Duke of Buckingham. Villiers had a lengthy tenure at the Stuart court, becoming an advisor to James's son and successor Charles I. He is the Duke of Buckingham in Alexandre Dumas's classic novel *The Three Musketeers*, who becomes embroiled in a passionate but unconsummated love affair with the queen of France, Anne of Austria, the wife of Louis XIII. That part is historically accurate. The 1st Duke of Buckingham, who was also Britain's Lord Admiral, maintained a shrine to Anne in his cabin aboard his flagship. He was stabbed to death in an English pub by a disgruntled sailor, angry over Buckingham's encouragement of Charles I to involve Britain in the Thirty Years' War.

The 2nd Duke of Buckingham (and second George Villiers) was a top advisor to Charles II and was best known for his sexcapades. He eloped with his wife, Mary, while the banns for her marriage to another man were already being read in church. And his cousin Barbara Villiers, Countess of Castlemaine and Duchess of Cleveland, titles earned on her back, was one of the king's most notorious and fecund mistresses, mother to five of his many royal bastards.

Harry and Meghan will also receive Scottish titles, just as William and Catherine did. The Duke and Duchess of Cambridge are also the Earl and Countess of Strathearn. The earldom of Ross is available, but it may bring bad luck. A former Earl of Ross was King Charles I, who was beheaded by his own people in January 1649 during England's civil war.

On HER WEDDING day, Meghan will become not only Princess Henry of Wales, a princess by marriage of the United Kingdom, Great Britain, and Northern Ireland, but either Her Royal Highness the Duchess of Clarence, HRH the Duchess of Sussex, or HRH the Duchess of Buckingham, in addition to any Scottish and Irish titles the Queen may bestow. Sussex would seem to be the ducal title that bears the least amount of baggage. Meghan would be the first-ever Duchess of Sussex, because the first duke's wife, Queen Victoria's aunt by marriage, was never granted that title. However, she will no longer be Meghan Markle, although people will likely continue to call her that, just as the Duchess of Cambridge is often referred to as Kate Middleton despite several years of marriage to William. After she becomes a royal, Meghan will sign her name as they do, with her first name only. Her new last name, if she chooses to use it, will be Mountbatten-Windsor, but the royals rarely use their surnames. Meghan's credit cards and driver's license will show her title as her name. And it remains to be seen how her passport situation will be handled, as it will take at least five years for Meghan to become a citizen of the UK. She doesn't get to jump the queue just because she is marrying the Queen's grandson.

Harry did earn a military promotion prior to his wedding. On Tuesday, December 19, 2017, after serving as Captain General Royal Marines for sixty-four years, Prince Philip stepped down from his role, and the Queen appointed Prince Harry to succeed him. Harry, who had already begun preparing for the position, accompanied his grandfather in his final duty as Captain General, as Their Royal Highnesses received the incoming and outgoing Commandants General at Buckingham Palace.

There will be a learning curve for Meghan when it comes to royal protocol, but even those born into the House of Windsor must learn such things as which utensil to use and when; and whom to bow and curtsy to according to the Order of Precedence, a list that itself should be committed to memory.

Meghan has perfected the wave that will not blur on camera, but will have to master the official way to enter and exit motorcars and helicopters, by bringing one leg to gracefully meet the other, keeping the knees together as much as possible; and "the duchess slant"—sitting in a chair with the legs closed and off to one side, so that photographers can't get a glimpse up her skirt. Other options when sitting are to keep her legs together or to cross them at the ankle. Meghan has been accustomed to being in the public eye, posing for cameras for the past several years, so it's highly unlikely that the royal family needs to worry that Harry's bride might get caught in any Britney Spears moments.

Even her older half sister Samantha admitted that Meghan was always "very classy, prim and proper, even when she was a child." Yet there are other arcane rules that Meghan will be expected to follow, including skirt length (no more minis) and natural-hued nail polish. Meghan nailed that one on November 27, 2017, during the engagement photo op when she showed off her ring.

Both the Queen and the Duchess of Cambridge have a go-to neutral shade that any woman who wishes to emulate them can find at her local drugstore: Essie's Ballet Slippers. In her wildest dreams, how could Essie Weingarten, a Jewish entrepreneur from Queens, New York, have imagined that the Queen of England would be wearing her nail polish!

It's also a requirement for women of Britain's royal family to wear pantyhose during official engagements. Meghan's bare legs on the day she and Harry appeared in KP's Sunken Garden to announce their engagement either broke or flouted protocol.

There were reports that Meghan would have to learn henceforth to speak the Queen's English. *Lavatory* should replace any synonyms; and from now on she should say *sofa* instead of *couch* (perhaps *couch* is what one does to one's words). In any event, if there really is a vocabulary list, it's not difficult for a professional actress to memorize a script.

Nevertheless, the notion than an American needs to learn to "tawk" properly smacks of the insults Catherine Middleton's mother received when she allegedly used the "wrong" (read: low class) vocabulary around the Queen, which the British toffs were certain would end any chances of Kate's ever wedding William.

Perhaps the most unusual preparation that Meghan had to undergo was military training, standard operating procedure for anyone marrying into the royal family. Memorizing which fork to use is nothing compared to learning what to do in case you are taken hostage. As part of her training exercises, Meghan might have been put through a simulation as if she were already a hostage and instructed on how to act when the room is stormed by the Special Air Service (SAS). She would have been taught how to slip out of zip ties and duct tape and how to convey information when she's under duress, using micro expressions and key words. Additional training would have included how to act without close protection—in other words, what to do if something goes horribly wrong and your protection officers are not able to do their duty.

Catherine Middleton underwent similar instruction before her marriage to Prince William; and even Diana and Prince Charles headed off on a secret mission to the Hereford headquarters of the SAS in 1993 for antiterrorist and kidnap training.

It's undoubtedly daunting to have to learn centuries of royal protocol within a brief space of time—the names, ranks, and duties of thousands of people, and what each tradition is on every occasion. But unlike Diana, or Catherine Middleton, who were nineteen years old when their respective royal relationships began, Meghan is thirty-six—an adult who enjoyed a successful career of her own before she met her prince. That career in front of the cameras, the red carpets and premieres, as well as appearing at charity and global events, have in part prepared her for public scrutiny, for being photographed all the time, and for being in the public eye. But the attention Meghan has had and will continue to receive as a young and beautiful royal is exponentially greater than she'd ever before experienced as a principal on a cable television series.

However, what may trip Meghan up is the very thing that makes her such a breath of fresh air to the royal family: her Americanism. During her January 2018 visit with Harry to Cardiff, Wales, Meghan reverted to Hollywood habits, breaking royal protocol by posing for a selfie with a teenage fan and signing an autograph, instead of politely declining, as members of the royal family are supposed to do. Yet she cleverly avoided the taboo of providing her signature by writing a cute message with a smiley face instead.

Moreover, Americans tend to be voluble, open books compared to the British. We love to share what we're feeling. Meghan blogged for three years about everything that was on her mind. Her followers knew all about her workout routines; her passions for yoga, Pilates, and running; her favorite chefs, restaurants, and recipes. Meghan posted the recipe for her favorite comfort food, her Grandma Markle's apple butter toast; and avid readers learned about the actress's obsession for a decadent winter warm-up, red wine hot chocolate. Not one to mince words, Meghan once described a pumpkin fondue as "the best f*cking thing I've ever eaten." If there really is a vocabulary list, then one of the words in that sentence may be on it, even though it was frequently used to great effect by Geoffrey Chaucer, a courtier to Meghan's purported ancestor King Edward III.

In The Tig, Meghan discussed her travels to far-flung getaways, her favorite flowers, and places to get a terrific facial, in addition to posting interviews with powerful women in various professions, essays about her philanthropic work, and excerpts from articles she had penned and speeches she had delivered on behalf of the nonprofit causes she both championed and worked with—"boots on the ground," in her words. Her Instagram feed had over three million followers. And her celebrity status afforded her the platform to speak about her humanitarian efforts with her fans and inspire them to become more involved with global and local causes.

Actors are accustomed to talking about what they are working on because promotion is part of the job. And most American actors don't mind doing publicity tours and being amusing on chat shows, whereas the opposite tends to be true of their British counterparts. Moreover, the royal family is not supposed to give interviews, except on rare occasions, or to display emotion in public. The former ruins the mystique and magic that cocoons the fairy-tale element of the monarchy, and the latter is considered vulgar. Yet during their interview with the BBC after the announcement of their engagement, Meghan certainly didn't dial back her effervescence or her obvious empathy for Harry when he spoke about his mother.

After Meghan marries Harry, she will also become a patron of the Royal Foundation of the Duke and Duchess of Cambridge and Harry, which serves as the main vehicle for their philanthropic activities. Meghan is already jumping with both feet into charitable endeavors. Her first official royal appearance was on World AIDS Day, December 1, when she toured Nottingham with Prince Harry. It was a perfect blend of activism for both of them. Diana was one of the first public figures to bring international awareness to the AIDS epidemic, and Harry has continued his mother's work with AIDS patients, researchers, and caregivers. For decades, AIDS has tragically and disproportionately affected members of the performing arts community as well.

Whether it was a rookie mistake or a declaration of independence, Meghan broke protocol during her first official engagement by carrying a handbag in Nottingham instead of a clutch. The Queen and the Duchess of Cambridge are always seen with clutches at such events. There is a method behind the madness. A lady can correctly hold a clutch in both hands, if necessary, which allows the royal to avoid shaking hands if she prefers not to.

In Nottingham, Meghan won the day, however. Just as merchants immediately sell out of whatever Prince William's wife or their children are wearing, an influence nicknamed the "Kate Effect," Meghan has the same magic.

Piggybacking their success with the fashion blog What Would Kate Do? Amanda Dishaw and Christine O'Brien-Ross launched a second blog titled Meghan's Mirror, which chronicles everything she wears, what it costs, and where her fans can purchase it. Meghan's influence, especially if she has children, is currently projected to top the financial impact of the Kate Effect, because Meghan has already been a fashion influencer in the United States and Canada for years, and her style is trendier, less traditional, and often more affordable than Kate's. In January 2018, Brand Finance estimated that Meghan's entry into the royal family could bring $677 million into Britain's economy in this calendar year alone, a figure that is only a reflection of her status as a style icon.

As an example, the $625 burgundy tricolor Strathberry Midi Tote Meghan wore on her arm in Nottingham (Harry was on the other arm) sold out within hours. The actual protocol-breaking purse Meghan carried that day was auctioned on eBay to benefit the Terrence Higgins Trust, which organized the World AIDS Day charity fair that she and Harry visited as part of their official royal tour.

It remains to be seen whether Meghan will ever resume her acting career. When she and Harry announced their engagement, she said at the time that because she had achieved success as an actress, she was comfortable starting a new chapter in her life and focusing solely on her philanthropic endeavors.

Grace Kelly was a decade younger than Meghan, with a Best Actress Oscar in her closet, when she wed Prince Rainier of Monaco. Believing she'd done it all by the age of twenty-five, she cheerfully gave up acting to marry a prince, only to regret it later. But that was the 1950s, and her husband, an old-school European Catholic who didn't think much of independent women, had always expected his wife to be no more than a mother and Monaco's most glamorous figurehead.

That's not Meghan and Harry, whom Meghan has referred to as a feminist, nor is the British monarchy, for all its hidebound traditions, Monaco in the 1950s.

No one is betting that Meghan will return to filming racy scenes in law office file rooms or lounging around in her lingerie. But might she narrate documentaries that focus on the charities supported by the Royal Foundation of the Duke and Duchess of Cambridge and Harry? Will a lifetime of attending philanthropic events and helping to raise funds for causes that are dear to her be enough?

Ribbon cutting has never been enough thus far for Harry. Both he and Meghan seek adventure as much as they seek to change the world for the better, and it will be exciting to see how the two of them transform and update the role of modern royals.

So what will Meghan's priorities be, once a ring is slipped on her finger in St. George's Chapel? Because Meghan will celebrate her thirty-seventh birthday three months after their marriage, will The Firm pressure her to become a mother right away, or will she and Harry be able to enjoy their lives together as newlyweds, allowing Meghan the time to acclimate herself to her new life in a new country? For centuries the first (and often only) obligation of a royal wife was to ensure the continuation of the dynasty by begetting an heir. Yet with each new Cambridge baby, Harry slides further down the line of succession. He adores children and has always said he would want them when the time is right. And he's finally found the right woman.

But given the fact that Meghan has been an independent professional in her own right for years, will she be able to call some of her own shots, or will her life be mapped out from now on by the Queen or the Men in Gray? Meghan has said, "I've never wanted to be a lady who lunches—I've always wanted to be a woman who works."

Harry still remains one of the most popular members of the royal family: the handsome, cheeky, charismatic man of the people; the rule breaker; the rebel with many causes. We live in an age of celebrity; and if Harry's mother was the people's princess, and William has said he aims to be the people's king, Harry is indeed the people's prince. And he is marrying a genuine celebrity in her own right, a woman who has already achieved what she desired in *two* careers—as an actress and as a humanitarian.

The couple's popularity appears boundless. When the announcement that America's Lifetime network had already greenlighted a cable TV movie of their romance made headline news across the world, websites as far from Kensington Palace as Qatar shared the production details. A pair of Meghan and Harry dolls in bridal finery retail for £131. And in perhaps the most unusual tribute, in January 2018, the London Zoo named its newborn okapi Meghan. Native to the Democratic Republic of the Congo, okapi, which are on the endangered species list, are members of the giraffe family, but don't have long necks. Meghan the okapi is black with zebra-like white stripes on her legs.

Royalty historian David Starkey put his finger on it when he noted that Meghan and Harry's union is "the first globalized royal marriage." She is "international in a way that no other royal has ever been; and her entry into the royal family will redefine her as much as she will redefine it, moving them one step closer to their people."

Yes, Meghan Markle is different from every royal bride in the history of the British monarchy. A biracial, childless divorcée in her mid-thirties, she is a college graduate with a double degree; and a self-described self-sufficient go-getter whose dual careers have in many ways prepared her for the spotlight, as well as for the public duties that will be required of her—as much as anything can truly prepare someone to become a member of the royal family if they are not born into it.

But Meghan Markle is something *else* that no other royal bride has ever been. She is a standard-bearer for all young women who have been told that it's impossible to "have it all."

Meghan completely embodies the incredible, utterly American female spirit of the "roll up your sleeves and get to work" *We Can Do It!* of the Rosie the Riveter poster on the wall of her childhood bedroom.

When it came to her racial identity or whether she was expected to decide to be an actress or a humanitarian, an independent woman or the wife of a prince, Meghan has *never* been either/or, but always fiercely, proudly *both*.

To all young women, especially those little girls, some of whom may be biracial, Meghan's life story thus far proclaims from the mountaintops that they *don't* have to choose between one parent or the other. They *can* be a glamorous actress *and* a powerful political activist and be just as successful in both endeavors. They can care just as much about flower arranging and fine wines as building wells in the dusty villages of Rwanda and helping adolescent girls in India—all to promote education and a lifetime of economic potential for every girl in the world. And P.S.: it isn't such a long shot to marry a foreign prince too, even when you're an American.

From now on a lot of girls from Staten Island to the San Fernando Valley will have their eyes on little Prince George of Cambridge!

Meghan has also been a role model for other young women and some not-so-young women by reminding all of us of the mantra she developed after too many casting directors told her she wasn't black or white enough to book a job or that she was "too" white or black to get the part. *You are enough*, she told herself. It was a message she spread through the gospel of The Tig and in the articles she penned online and for print magazines. "I never let my relationship [with Prince Harry] define me," Meghan told a prominent periodical. In February 2017, under a post titled "Be Your Own Valentine," she reminded women that they did not need to define themselves by others or live their lives through them. They needed to take the time to honor themselves. "I think you need to cook that beautiful dinner when it's just you. Wear your favorite outfit, buy yourself some flowers, and celebrate the self-love that often gets muddled when we focus on what we don't have."

Harry and Meghan's story is that of two children whose parents separated when they were very young and who lived separate lives with each parent and a third life with both parents.

It's the story of a boy who lost his beautiful and glamorous mother—the most famous woman in the world—when he was on the cusp of adolescence and needed her most. He spent decades trying to find himself, and often found himself at the center of scandal instead.

From Harry's own revelations about sorting out his mental health issues when he was in his late twenties, he had to come to terms with his mother's tragic death, get past his anger, and process his mourning for her before he could heal. How could he have a healthy relationship with anyone when he was so emotionally wounded? Therapists like to tell their clients "you can't love someone else until you love yourself."

And how could Harry be open to *finding* The One until he found himself? Playboy princes make great tabloid fodder but radioactive husbands.

At the time of her engagement and wedding to Prince Harry, Meghan was the same age as Harry's mother Diana was when she died.

Somehow it seems appropriate to give Diana the last word, because Harry has wanted her to be a part of his journey with Meghan from the start. It was why he repurposed two of his mother's diamonds into Meghan's engagement ring. Diana, who consulted spiritualists, psychics, and mediums and who once shocked the former Buckingham Palace press secretary Dickie Arbiter by telling him that she'd always known she was being watched over by the spirits of her ancestors, would surely believe that she is indeed looking down on Harry and Meghan from some astral plane.

Diana once said that "royal firstborns get all the glory, but second-borns enjoy more freedom. Only when Harry is a lot older will he realize how lucky he is not to have been the eldest." In many ways, because William has always had his life mapped out for him, Harry has had more freedom to define his role within the royal family. At times it's been as much of a curse as it's been a blessing.

When Harry was eight years old and William ten, Diana gave them the proverbial talk about the birds and the bees. A blushing Harry fled the room, but one suspects he did hear his mother's marital advice, because William certainly did. Diana told her sons, whether or not your bride is royal, "if she is the person you truly love, then that's all that matters."

It's as delightfully old-fashioned as it's thoroughly modern.

May Harry and Meghan live happily ever after.

# *Acknowledgments*

Because current events have moved at supersonic speed, I have a village to thank for the spectacular haste with which this book had to be written and produced. First, to my agent, Irene Goodman, who believed me from the start when I told her that Harry and Meghan would get engaged and that their very coupledom was newsworthy. To my editor and fellow fan of all things British monarchy, Rachel Kahan; to Jen Hart, queen of Morrow paperbacks; and to the phenomenal art department and my PR team at William Morrow, Anwesha Basu, Bianca Flores, and Amelia Wood. To Margaret Evans Porter, my C of E Sherpa and fact-checker, for her astute suggestions; and whose eagle eye caught me drifting from royal weddings into *Four Weddings and a Funeral*, saving me from a disastrously laughable Freudian slip of the fingers. To Elizabeth Kerri Mahon and Kirsten Erickson McElroy for keeping me posted on the steady stream of news flashes from both sides of the pond as I wrote like the wind. Thanks to Susan Wald for her spot-on "acorn" remark. To Teri Gilman for her long and exhaustive hours of genealogy research; and to Jordan Auslander for helping to delve into the mystery of whether Meghan *might* have had a Jewish ancestress. To my grandparents for encouraging me to become an Anglophile, an actress, and an author. To my royal-watching mother from Beverly Hills, who as a starry-eyed teen avidly followed Princess Margaret's ill-fated romance; and who also permitted me to wear her souvenir tiara from Harry's grandmother's coronation onstage; and to my father, my real-life Robert Zane: thank you for getting it. And—always—to my husband, Scott: not only for providing perspective on the in-country experience in Afghanistan but for being kind, patient, loving, and supportive, no matter what. Scott and I share a wedding day with Meghan and Harry, so I have a feeling that they too will forever be just as lucky in love!

# Selected Bibliography

Below is a list of volumes used to research this book, as well as suggested reading for those who wish to delve deeper into other Windsor marriages and the royal affairs and marriages of past British dynasties. It's also a reading list for those who wish to know more about how far the British monarchy has come with regard to the issue of divorce, as well as the topics of marriage to Catholics and the royals of the past who had romantic relationships with prominent actresses.

Andersen, Christopher. *William and Kate: A Royal Love Story*. New York: Gallery Books, 2011.

Aronson, Theo. *Princess Margaret: A Biography*. London: Michael O'Mara Books Limited, 1997. [chapter 23 copyright 2001]

Bedell Smith, Sally. *Prince Charles: The Passions and Paradoxes of an Improbable Life*. New York: Random House, 2017.

Birmingham, Stephen. *Duchess: The Story of Wallis Warfield Simpson*. Boston: Little, Brown, 1981.

Bradford, Sarah. *George VI*. London: Penguin Books, 2011.

Brand, Emily. *Royal Weddings*. Great Britain: Shire Publications, 2011.

Brown, Tina. *The Diana Chronicles*. New York: Doubleday, 2007.

Cawthorne, Nigel. *Sex Lives of the Kings and Queens of England*. London: Prion, 1994.

Coxe, Howard. *The Stranger in the House: A Life of Caroline of Brunswick*. London: Chatto & Windus, 1939.

David, Saul. *Prince of Pleasure: The Prince of Wales and the Making of the Regency*. New York: Atlantic Monthly Press, 1998.

Denny, Joanna. *Katherine Howard: A Tudor Conspiracy*. London: Portrait/Piatkus Books, Ltd., 2005.

Feuchtwanger, Edgar. *Albert and Victoria: The Rise and Fall of the House of Saxe-Coburg-Gotha*. London: Hambledon Continuum, 2006.

Fraser, Antonia, ed. *The Lives of the Kings & Queens of England*, revised and updated. Berkeley: University of California Press, 1998.

Fraser, Antonia. *Royal Charles: Charles II and the Restoration*. New York: Alfred A. Knopf, 1979.

Fraser, Flora. *The Unruly Queen: The Life of Queen Caroline*. New York: Alfred A. Knopf, 1996.

Heald, Tim. *Princess Margaret: A Life Unravelled*. London: Phoenix, 2008.

Hewitt, James. *Love and War*. London: Blake Publishing, Ltd., 1999.

Hibbert, Christopher. *Edward VII: The Last Victorian King*. New York: St. Martin's Griffin, 2007.

——. *George IV: The Rebel Who Would Be King*. New York: St. Martin's Griffin, 2007.

——. *Queen Victoria: A Personal History*. New York: HarperCollins, 2000.

——. *Queen Victoria in Her Letters and Journals*. New York: Viking Penguin, 1985.

Higham, Charles. *The Duchess of Windsor: The Secret Life*. Hoboken, NJ: John Wiley, 1988.

Holme, Thea. *Caroline: A Biography of Caroline of Brunswick*. New York: Atheneum, 1980.

Irvine, Valerie. *The King's Wife: George IV and Mrs. Fitzherbert*. London: Hambledon and London, 2005.

Ives, Eric. *The Life and Death of Anne Boleyn*, 2nd ed. Oxford: Blackwell Publishing, 2004.

James, Susan. *Catherine Parr: Henry VIII's Last Love*. Stroud, Gloucestershire: Tempus Publishing, 2008.

Joseph, Claudia. *Kate: Kate Middleton: Princess in Waiting*. New York: Avon Books, 2009.

Junor, Penny. *Charles: Victim or Villain?* New York: HarperCollins, 1998.

King, Greg. *The Duchess of Windsor: The Uncommon Life of Wallis Simpson*. New York: Citadel Press, 2000.

Lamont-Brown, Raymond. *Alice Keppel & Agnes Keyser: Edward VII's Last Loves*. Thrupp, Stroud, Gloucestershire: Sutton Publishing, 1998.

Larcombe, Duncan. *Prince Harry: The Inside Story*. London: HarperCollins, 2017.

Leslie, Anita. *Mrs. Fitzherbert*. New York: Scribner, 1960.

Mattingly, Garrett. *Catherine of Aragon*. New York: Book-of-the-Month Club, 1941.

Moody, Marcia. *Harry: A Biography*. London: Michael O'Mara Books Ltd, 2014.

Morton, Andrew. *Diana, Her True Story* [A Commemorative Edition with New Material Including *Her Own Words*], revised 25th anniversary ed. New York: Simon & Schuster, 1997/2017.

Munson, James. *Maria Fitzherbert: The Secret Wife of George IV*. New York: Carroll & Graf Publishers, 2001.

Nicholl, Katie. *William and Harry: Behind the Palace Walls*. New York: Weinstein Books, 2010.

Plowden, Alison. *Caroline and Charlotte: Regency Scandals*. Thrupp, Stroud, Gloucestershire: Sutton Publishing, 2005.

Shawcross, William. *The Queen Mother: The Official Biography*. New York: Vintage Books, 2010.

Starkey, David. *Six Wives: The Queens of Henry VIII*. New York: HarperCollins, 2003.

Weir, Alison. *The Six Wives of Henry VIII*. New York: Grove Press, 1991.

Williams, Neville. *The Tudors,* ed. Antonia Fraser. Berkeley: University of California Press, 2000.

Williams, Susan. *The People's King: The True Story of the Abdication.* New York: Palgrave Macmillan, 2004.

Wilson, A. N. *The Rise & Fall of the House of Windsor.* New York and London: W. W. Norton, 1993.

Wilson, Christopher. *A Greater Love: Prince Charles's Twenty-Year Affair with Camilla Parker Bowles.* New York: William Morrow, 1994.

———. *The Windsor Knot: Charles, Camilla and the Legacy of Diana.* New York: Citadel Press, 2002.

# About the Author

Native New Yorker Leslie Carroll is the author of twenty books in three genres (as well as a contributor to a twenty-first book with an essay on how she met her husband while he was serving in Afghanistan). Among her published titles are a series of five nonfiction volumes on the loves and lives of European royalty. She also wrote the text for an illustrated coffee-table book on a thousand years of British royalty commissioned by Sterling, the publishing arm of Barnes & Noble. Her titles have been translated into eleven languages; and some of her novels have been optioned for TV and motion pictures. Leslie is considered to be one of America's experts on European royalty and is a frequent media presence whenever the House of Windsor marks a milestone. She flew to London for the royal wedding of Prince William and Catherine Middleton, and provided numerous eyewitness interviews that day for print and radio, from *The Wall Street Journal* to the Canadian Broadcasting Corporation, among others. Leslie has had multiple appearances on the Travel Channel, Rick Steves's travel show, and Canada's History Channel series as an expert speaking about various controversial royals. The *Chicago Tribune* has described her historical nonfiction as "an irresistible combination of *People* magazine and the History Channel." A professional actress who had a survival job for years as a real-life Rachel Zane,

Leslie is also an award-winning audiobook narrator, specializing in bringing historical fiction alive for the listener. On her paternal grandmother's side, she is a descendant of Nathan Marcus Adler, Chief Rabbi of the British empire during the reign of Queen Victoria. Visit her at www.lesliecarroll.com.